about
Children
and
Sport

Advice for Parents, Coaches, and Teachers

Coaching Association of Canada

M

Mosaic Press
Oakville, ON. - Buffalo, N.Y.

Straight Talk

about

Children

and

Sport

Advice for Parents, Coaches, and Teachers

Written by
Janet LeBlanc and Louise Dickson

Sponsored by

 ROYAL BANK OF CANADA
CHARITABLE FOUNDATION

For more information about the programs and services of the Coaching Association of Canada or the National Coaching Program, please contact:

Coaching Association of Canada
141 Laurier Avenue West,
Suite 300, Ottawa, Ontario
K1P 5J3
Tel: (613)235-5000 Fax: (613)235-9500
coach@coach.ca
www.coach.ca

Canadian Cataloguing in Publication Data

LeBlanc, Janet E., 1959-
Straight talk about children and sport: advice for parents, coaches and teachers
Includes bibliographical references.
ISBN 0-88962-630-8
1. Sports for children 2. Sports for children - Psychological aspects. I. Dickson, Louise, 1959-
II. Coaching Association of Canada III. Title.
GV709.2.L42   1997   796.01922   C96-901006-0

Co-Published by Mosaic Press and the Coaching Association of Canada.
Mosaic Press acknowledges the financial support of the Canada Council, the Ontario Arts Council and the Department of Canadian Heritage, Government of Canada.

The programs of the Coaching Association of Canada are financially supported by Sport Canada, Government of Canada.

Mosaic Press in Canada
1252 Speers Road
Units 1&2
Oakville, Ontario
L6L 5N9
Tel/Fax: (905) 825-2130
Editorial:
cp507@freenet.toronto.on.ca
Orders & Service:
mosaicpress@aibn.com

Mosaic Press in the U.S.A.
PMB 145
4500 Witmer Industrial Estates
Niagara Falls, NY
14305-1386
Tel/Fax: 1-800-387-8992
Editorial:
cp507@freenet.toronto.on.ca
Orders & Service:
mosaicpress@aibn.com

Many of the photographs included in this publication are courtesy of *The Ottawa Citizen*, National Sport Organizations and Canadian Sport Images.

Edited by: Sheila Robertson
Layout and Design by: Aerographics Creative Services
Cover Photo: *The Ottawa Citizen*
Back Cover Photo: F. Scott Grant
Page Three Photos (L to R): CAHPERD, J. LeBlanc, L. Hendry

Printed and bound in Canada.

Preface

Straight Talk About Children And Sport provides some important information about the early developmental needs of young children in organized sport. It focuses on children between the ages of six and 12 years, a time when they are most likely to be introduced to sport. Because all children develop at different times and at different rates, the ages used in the book are provided only as a general guideline.

Straight Talk About Children And Sport has been written using a two-page question-and-answer format. Each answer provides a rationale, some background information, and expands on related themes. *Straight Talk* was designed to provide a brief overview of some of the latest research in the area of children in sport. It does not attempt to fully represent the extensive research that has been conducted in this field.

Their first introduction to sport leaves a lasting impression on children. I hope that this book will give parents, coaches, and teachers some direction on how to make the experience enjoyable, fostering a love of sport that will continue throughout their lives.

Janet LeBlanc, M.B.A.
Coaching Association of Canada

Acknowledgments

Straight Talk About Children And Sport was made possible with a grant from the Royal Bank Charitable Foundation. On behalf of the Coaching Association of Canada, I extend my sincere and grateful appreciation to the Foundation for its generous financial support. I would also like to thank Alain Marion for his significant contribution to the development of this book, to Mary Woods for her expert proofreading, to David O'Malley and Alex Moyes for their creativity, to Sheila Robertson for her consistent editing, to Geoff Gowan for his leadership, and a special word of thanks to Tim Robinson for his guidance and support. Thanks are also due to the many committed professionals whose expertise and years of research have made this book possible.

Janet

Contributors

Oded Bar-Or, M.D., Professor of Pediatrics, McMaster University

Marilyn Booth, Sport Nutrition Program Director, Sport Medicine and Science Council of Canada

David Carmichael, M.A., Director of Research and Development, The Ontario Physical and Health Education Association

Geoff Gowan, Ph.D., Former President, Coaching Association of Canada

Lorraine Hendry, B.Sc. (PT), Director of Physiotherapy, Physio Sports Care Centre; Director of Physiotherapy, University of Ottawa Sports Medicine Centre

Kathryn Keely, M.D., Pediatrician, Clinical Practice; Canadian representative to the Committee on Sports Medicine and Fitness of the American Academy of Pediatrics

William MacIntyre, M.D., Orthopedic Surgeon, Children's Hospital of Eastern Ontario

Alain Marion, M.Sc., Consultant, Coaching Association of Canada

Terry Orlick, Ph.D., Professor, School of Human Kinetics, University of Ottawa

Michel Portmann, Ph.D., Professeur, Département de Kinanthropologie, Université du Québec à Montréal

Keith Russell, Ph.D., Associate Professor, College of Physical Education, University of Saskatchewan

Stuart Robbins, Ph.D., Chair of the School of Physical Education, York University

Glyn Roberts, Ph.D., Sport Psychologist, Institute of Child Behavior and Development, University of Illinois

Lyle Sanderson, M.Sc., Associate Professor, College of Physical Education, University of Saskatchewan

Ken Shields, M.PhEd., President, Commonwealth Centre for Sport Development; President, Canadian Professional Coaches Association

Roy Shephard, M.D. (Lond.), Ph.D., D.P.E., Professor Emeritus of Applied Physiology, School of Physical and Health Education, University of Toronto

Murray Smith, Ph.D., Sport Psychologist, Clinical Practice

Geraldine Van Gyn, Ph.D., Associate Professor, School of Physical Education, University of Victoria

Foreword

Congratulations! By reading this book you have taken a very important first step towards ensuring that children enjoy positive experiences in sport. As a parent, coach, or teacher, you have enormous responsibility with respect to the types of experiences youngsters will encounter in the sport environment.

Much of the content of *Straight Talk About Children And Sport* may be familiar to you because it offers commonsense advice. However, as we are frequently reminded, there is nothing common about commonsense!

The topics were selected because the questions are ones that a parent, coach, or teacher *should* ask. The answers get right to the point and provide the basis for sound decision-making.

Straight Talk can be read at one sitting, but should be referred to whenever questions arise. Similar topics are clustered, so examining a single important question may lead you to further exploration of related issues.

If you want to do more reading on a topic, consult the reference at the end of each section. And if you encounter difficulty following up on any references, please contact the Coaching Association of Canada for assistance.

It is my hope that this extremely useful book will be read by thousands of others just like you. If you — and they — apply only half the contents, multitudes of Canadian children will benefit.

Geoff Gowan

Geoff Gowan, C.M., Ph.D.

Contents

Part Three   How Children Grow and Develop

Part Four   The Mind of a Child

Part Five Sport Injuries in Young Children

Part Six The Role of Parents and Coaches in Sport

Part One

Children and Sport: An Introduction

Why is sport important for children? ▶

The Ottawa Citizen

◀C hildren have to be active every day. Physical activity stimulates growth and leads to improved physical and emotional health. Today, research shows that the importance of physical activity in children is stronger than ever. For example, medical researchers have observed that highly active children are less likely to suffer from high blood pressure, diabetes, cancer of the colon, obesity, and coronary heart disease later in life.

Exercise is also known to relieve stress. Some children experience as much stress, depression, and anxiety as adults do. And because exercise improves health, a fit child is more likely to be well-rested and mentally sharp. Even moderate physical activity has been shown to improve a child's skill at arithmetic, reading, and memorization.

But sport, not just exercise, gives a child more than just physical well-being; it contributes to a child's development both psychologically and socially. Sport psychologist Dr. Glyn Roberts of the University of Illinois has worked primarily in children's sport for the last two decades. He emphasizes that sport is an important learning environment for children.

"Sport can affect a child's development of self-esteem and self-worth," explains Roberts. "It is also within sport that peer status and peer acceptance is established and developed."

One way children gain acceptance by their peers is to be good at activities valued by other children, says Roberts. Research shows that children would rather play sports than do anything else. A study conducted in the United States showed that high school boys and girls would rather be better at sports than in academic subjects. The same study showed that high school boys would rather fail in class than be incompetent on the playing field.

Because sport is important to children, being good at sports is a strong social asset. Young boys in particular use sports and games to measure themselves against their friends. Children who are competent at sports are more easily accepted by children of their own age, and are more likely to be team captains and group leaders. Such children usually have better social skills.

The primary goal of parents and coaches is to help children find the success in sport they need to make them feel valued and wanted. Every child can be successful at one sport or another. Take the time to find the sports that are right for each child.

What does success mean to a child?▶

◀C hildren don't think like adults. They view success differently and these views differ with age, gender, and the type of sport they play. British researcher Dr. Jean Whitehead asked 3,000 youngsters aged nine to 16 years to describe what success in sport means to them. She received these answers from primary school children.

> *"I did my first back dive ever in front of my brother and my dad."*
> *"I swam a length with nobody helping me."*
> *"We were practising and I was the only one who could do it."*
> *"I practised and practised, then one day I did it!"*[1]

These replies show that children don't see winning as the only kind of success. In fact, winning is most often cited last when children are asked about their reasons for participating.

In an article in *Coaching Children in Sport* entitled "Why Children Choose to do Sport — or Stop", author Whitehead writes: "Young children are more concerned with mastering their own environment and developing skills than with beating others — at least until someone tells them that it is important to win."

Up to about age 10, children believe that success and doing well are based upon effort and social approval. Because their capacity to assess their own ability develops very slowly, they cannot have clear expectations about how successful they will be in sport. They believe that those who try hard are successful, and if you are successful, you must have tried hard. Children in this age bracket tend to think of success as finishing the race, regardless of whether they placed first, second, or 20th.

At about six to seven years of age, children start to compare their skills with other children. They start to wonder whether others can do the same things they can. Things that are 'hard' are those few others can do. It is not until about 12 years of age that children are able to tell the difference between skill, luck, effort, and true athletic ability.

Because children are not good at judging their own ability, they depend on others to tell them how well they are doing in developing skills and how they compare with their peers. This places enormous responsibility on parents and coaches not to set standards that are too high.

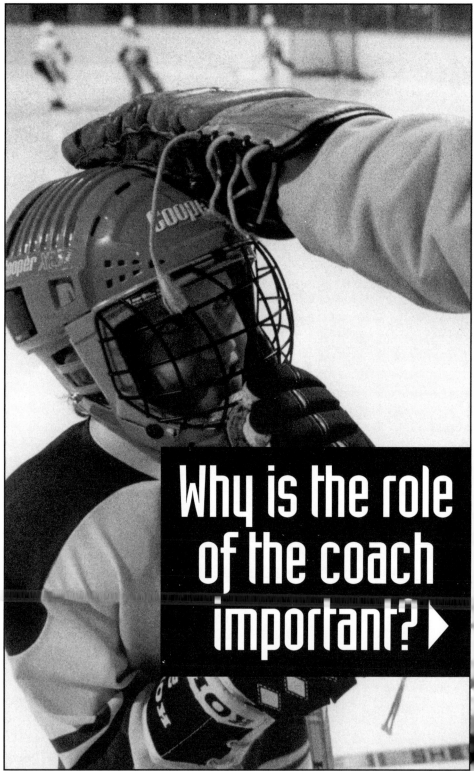

Why is the role of the coach important? ▶

Pre-adolescent children are barometers of the reaction of adults, says sport psychologist Dr. Glyn Roberts. Because they are unable to assess their own abilities, children rely on what grown-ups say and do to interpret their experiences. By their cheers and looks of approval or disapproval, parents and coaches pass judgment on a child's ability and performance. In the process, they play an important role in shaping children's perception of themselves.

The way in which a coach corrects a skill, reinforces a behaviour, or highlights an error plays an important role in either developing or impairing the self-esteem of young athletes. A study conducted in Québec found that 96 per cent of youngsters say their coach plays an important role in influencing their behaviour, compared to 65 per cent for teachers and 55 per cent for parents. Good coaches recognize the important role they play in influencing behaviour and boosting the confidence and self-esteem of their young charges.

Raising the confidence of young children means building on strengths rather than weaknesses. Good coaching is based on a positive approach and follows these commonsense principles.

Provide plenty of sincere praise when children are learning and refining new physical skills. Some researchers suggest giving three or four positive or encouraging statements, then offering some technical instruction, advice, or correction.
Use a 'sandwich' approach to correcting mistakes. By providing technical instruction sandwiched between two positive and encouraging statements, parents and coaches will focus on a child's strengths rather than weaknesses.
Develop realistic expectations that are based on individual abilities. Don't expect children to perform as miniature adults.
Reward correct techniques, not just outcomes. For some children, winning may be an unlikely achievement.
Reward effort as much as outcome.
Teach children how to strive to win by giving maximum effort.[2]

"Every Athlete Deserves a Certified Coach."

Slogan of the
National Coaching Certification Program

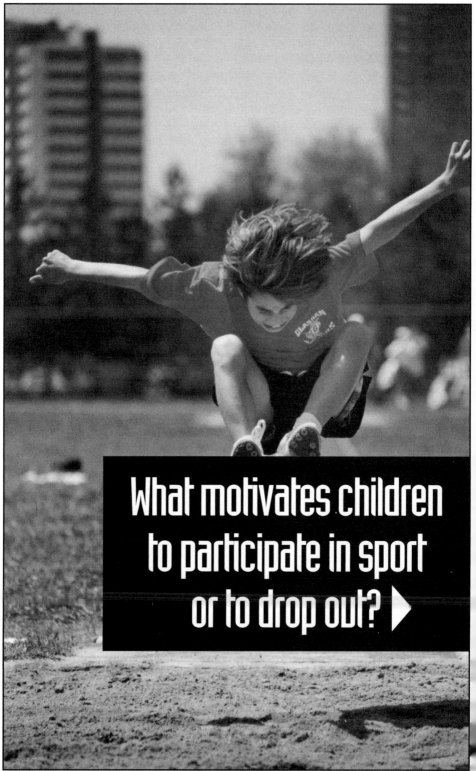

What motivates children to participate in sport or to drop out? ▶

U nderstanding why children participate in sport is not a simple matter. One of the difficulties is that children have many reasons for getting involved, and some of their reasons change from day to day. To encourage children to stay involved in sport, parents and coaches must understand these reasons.

In general, children participate in sport in order to have fun, improve skills, belong to a group, be successful, gain recognition, get fit, and find excitement. Conversely, they drop out of sport because of other interests, boredom, lack of success, too much pressure, loss of interest, friends leaving, or because it ceases to be fun.

Dr. Terry Orlick, professor of sport psychology at the University of Ottawa, says children play sport because it makes them feel good. They need to feel wanted, valued, and joyful. But if he or she is suddenly benched or pulled from the line-up because the team needs to win, a child might feel incompetent and rejected.

Children don't join a team to sit around and do nothing. Sport is not enjoyable if they don't get much opportunity to play. Studies have shown that children would rather play for a losing team than be members of a winning team and sit on the sidelines. If they're not playing, they'll lose interest very quickly.

A 1992 study conducted by Dr. Martha Ewing and Dr. Vern Seefeldt of the Institute for the Study of Youth Sports at Michigan State University asked 26,000 students aged 10 to 18 years about their reasons for participating in sport, why they quit, and how they feel about winning. The study found that 'fun' is the pivotal reason for being in sport — and lack of fun is a leading reason for dropping out. In fact, both boys and girls say that making practices more fun is the most important change they would make in a sport they dropped.

"It is interesting to note that even top athletes quit their very lucrative careers when sport is no longer fun."

Dr. Stuart Robbins
Former national level soccer coach

How can
sport be
more fun? ▶

Sport provides children with an opportunity to succeed by learning new skills or accomplishing new tasks. When young children enter the sporting world, they often learn new skills quite quickly. Some, for example, will show up at the first practice unable to catch a ball or throw accurately. A week later, they'll be catching the ball most of the time and throwing fairly well. Children who see themselves improving can gain a lot of satisfaction from playing. For some, sport may be the sole opportunity for success in a difficult childhood.

Dr. Steven Danish, director of the Life Skills Centre and professor of psychology at Virginia Commonwealth University, believes fun in sport comes from *balancing* challenge and skill. Enjoyment is highest when people set their *own* challenges and assess their performance against these challenges. The reward comes from competing against your own potential and goals, not from a competition over which you have little control.

To reinforce this point, Edmonton sport psychologist Dr. Murray Smith suggests watching young skateboarders at play. "This activity can be dangerous and requires a high level of skill," says Smith. "Virtually none of the children get hurt because they are in control of the risks they take and can decide for themselves when they are ready to go to the next stage."

Children need to be challenged, but if a game or activity is too overwhelming, a child might become anxious and not want to play anymore. On the other hand, when children are forced to repeat drills endlessly and pressured to become so proficient that they are not being challenged, boredom sets in.

Fun in Sports: A Balance between Skill and Challenge[3]

Skill	**ENJOYMENT**	Challenge

Challenge / Skill

BOREDOM / ANXIETY

Skill / Challenge

When skill outweighs challenge, boredom may result, leading to dropping out.

When the challenge outweighs skill, anxiety may result, leading to dropping out.

Does sport
build
character?▶

Dr. Stuart Robbins, chair of the School of Physical Education at York University in North York, Ont., says that sport is inherently neither good nor bad. The positive and negative effects associated with sport do not result from participation but from the *nature* of the experience.

In the hands of the right people with the right attitudes, sport can be a positive, character-building experience. It provides one of the best opportunities for children to come in contact with rules and social values. It defines the need to get along well with others and be accepted as part of a team. It plays a prime role in promoting values such as tolerance, fairness, and responsibility.

With proper leadership, sport provides the opportunity for children to
- acquire an appreciation for an active lifestyle
- develop a positive self-image by mastering sport skills
- learn to work as part of a team
- develop social skills with other children and adults
- learn about managing success and disappointment
- learn respect for others.[4]

The idea that sport builds character comes from 19th-century Britain where many believed the playing fields were the training ground for the discipline necessary to produce leaders in adult life. Physical activity, they thought, was a social experience that powerfully influenced attitudes and values.

The key virtue the British tried to instill in young people through sport was a sense of fairness and justice. Following rules, respecting your opponent, not cheating, and learning how to be good winners and losers were considered by headmasters to be part of what it meant to be a good citizen. Their philosophy was not to play for external rewards like money or fame, because that would tend to make one act unfairly.[5]

The notion that sport builds character does not sit well with today's critics of competitive sport. The external pressures of high profits and high salaries have often led to the corruption of these ideals. Instead of building character, competitive sport, which values winning above all else, challenges this notion. The more important winning becomes, the more the rewards for fair play and other values are likely to be diminished.

How can parents
and coaches
help children to
handle defeat? ▶

I n every sport contest there are winners and losers. In fact, when winning is narrowly defined as placing first, second, or third, there are usually more losers than winners. Handling defeat is one of the important lessons that young children can learn through sport.

Adults who organize and supervise a sport program play an important role in creating positive lessons about winning and losing. For example, coaches who are continually 'bending' the rules in order to win are likely to teach children that cheating is acceptable. Children who work with coaches who play by the rules will learn a different view of morality.

Ken Shields, former national men's basketball coach, says that "the time to teach youngsters important values such as the spirit of competition and how to cope with defeat is in their formative years. They need to be taught at an early age how to celebrate accomplishments even if they don't win the competition. Coaches play a very important role in shaping the environment of children."

Parents and coaches can teach youngsters how to cope with defeat by keeping losing in perspective. Remind them that every athlete loses at one time or another — even superstars.

Minimizing criticism also helps children to cope with defeat. When children lose, they don't need to be reminded about the loss. They should be rewarded for their attempt and reminded that everyone can learn important lessons from every defeat.

Sometimes children are put in situations where success may be next to impossible. Sport organizers, unfortunately, tend to group children according to chronological age rather than by size and weight. Through no fault of his or her own, one child may not be as mature physically or mentally as another, making it difficult to master a particular skill or to win a competition.

"The coach's job is to structure and fine-tune workouts to produce a guaranteed success. Athletes succeed on success."

Dr. Doug Clement
Olympic athletics coach
Success Stories

Are children miniature adults? ▶

Of course not. But a lot of parents seem to think they are.

The mistake is easy to make when a five-year-old child, barely able to skate, is decked out in $500 worth of hockey equipment, trying to play an adult game by adult rules under the supervision of an official. The mistake is easy to make when a nine-year-old figure skater jumps and twirls her way across the ice, sporting a high-cut costume covered in rhinestones and sequins.

Dressing our children to resemble professional athletes makes it hard to remember that a kid is just a kid. And many parents make the mistake of thinking children's sport is a miniature version of adult sport.

Dr. Murray Smith warns parents that adult sporting situations may be inappropriate, even harmful, to children. The way adults learn, play, and organize sport is not necessarily suitable for children. One reason is that children think differently from adults. Their minds are not fully developed and they are not equipped to make complex decisions or solve more than the simplest problems.

The classic example is 'beehive soccer.' Immediately following the free pass, 20 pairs of legs are within 10 yards of the ball, behaving like a swarm of bees following their queen. Meanwhile, there are sideline pleas to "stay in position" and "get back to where you belong."

Beehive soccer is the result of kids just being kids. The concept of 'teamwork' involves a set of relationships too complex for young children to grasp. When youngsters cluster around a ball, they are all playing as individuals. To play a team game, children must understand the rules and their tasks as members of the team. They must also understand the tasks of all the other team members. At a young age, these concepts are often too abstract for children.

Games should be modified to correspond to a child's level of development. Changing the rules of play to suit the developmental age of the players, and stressing fun and skill development more than the final outcome, will make sport more suitable for children.

How can parents and coaches keep sport and winning in perspective? ▶

In general, children tend to keep sport in perspective. At the end of a game, many children don't know if they've won or lost. While parents and coaches may dwell on the result of a competition, a child will go home and forget about it. According to a *USA Today/NBC* telephone poll, almost three out of four children aged 10 to 17 years said they wouldn't care if no score was kept during a game.

The tendency to value winning above all else has been recognized as the cause of many problems in children's sport. When winning is kept in perspective, the focus is more accurately placed on *striving* to win and the *pursuit* of victory. Successful coaches recognize that teaching children how to master new skills and strive for excellence even if they risk an error will produce children who can compete against others and feel good about themselves.

Keeping sport in perspective also means balancing a child's sport interest with a variety of other life activities. When children spend 20 hours a week in a pool or gymnasium, they do not have time for music classes, socializing with friends, or attending cultural events. Children should be taught at an early age that being active in sport is one part of a healthy lifestyle allowing for a balance between sport and other interests.

Dr. Geoff Gowan, former president of the Coaching Association of Canada, says keeping sport in perspective also means introducing children to a vast variety of sport experiences. "It's important that they are involved in a little bit of hockey, a little bit of baseball, a little bit of soccer, and a little bit of gymnastics," says Gowan. "This helps to take the pressure off youngsters and teaches them that the essence of sport is simply participation."

Introducing children to different sports will help them to develop running, jumping, throwing, catching, kicking, swinging, and pulling skills — the fundamental skills of human movement. When children build a base of sports skills, they are really building a launching platform for the future, says Gowan.

Parents should also give serious thought to guiding their children towards activities they can play throughout their lives. Sports such as swimming, bicycling, skiing, and soccer can be enjoyed by people of all ages. Some of the highly strenuous collision sports can be enjoyed by lots of participants, but may not lend themselves to a lifetime of injury-free play.

Reference Notes

1   Whitehead, J. (1993) Why children choose to do sport—or stop. *Coaching Children in Sport*. London: E&FN SPON. p. 110.
2   Petlichkoff, L. (1994/95) Introductory philosophy: developing the appropriate objectives in sport. *Coaching Focus*. 27, (Winter), pp. 3-4.
3   Danish, S. (1990) *American youth and sports participation*. Athletic Footwear Association. Florida: American Youth Sports Foundation. p. 7.
4   American Sport Education Program. (1994) *SportParent*. Champaign: Human Kinetics. p. 4.
5   Todd, D. (1996) Sports: the games we play promote everyday values. *The Ottawa Citizen*. Saturday, April 27th.

References

Almond, C. (1993) Physical activity levels in children—the implications for physical education. *Physical Activity in the Lifecycle: Proceedings*. Wingate Institute: Israel. pp. 117-125.

American Sport Education Program. (1994) *SportParent*. Champaign: Human Kinetics. p. 4.

DeMarco, T. & Sidney, K. (1989) Enhancing children's participation in physical activity. *Journal of School Health*. 59 (8), pp. 337-340.

Deshaies, P., Vallerand, R., Guerrier, J.P. (1984) *La connaissance et l'attitude des jeunes sportifs Québécois face à l'esprit sportif*. Québec: À la Régie de la sécurité dans les sports du Québec.

Dodd, M. (1990) Children say having fun is no. 1. *USA Today*. September 10th.

Duda, J.L. (1992) Motivation in sport settings: a goal perspective approach. *Motivation in Sport and Exercise* (ED. G.C. Roberts). Champaign: Human Kinetics. pp. 57-92.

Evans, J., Roberts, G.C. (1987) Physical competence and the development of children's peer relations. *Quest*. 39, pp. 23-35.

Fishburne, G., Harper-Tarr, D.A. (1990) An analysis of the typical elementary school timetable: a concern for health and fitness, sport and physical activity. *The Proceedings of the AIESEP World Convention*, (July), London: E&FN SPON. pp. 362-375.

Grace, N. (1987) Sports medicine section position paper: school physical education program. *Ontario Medical Review*. (March) pp. 218-221.

Keays, J. (1993) *The effects of regular (moderate to vigorous) physical activity in the school setting on students' health, fitness, cognition, psychological development, academic performance and classroom behaviour*. North York: North York Community Health Promotion Research Unit.

Martens, R. (1985) Coaching philosophy—winning and success. *Coaching Focus*. National Coaching Foundation. Autumn. 2, p. 16.

Orlick, T. (1974) The athletic dropout—a high price for inefficiency. *Canadian Association of Health, Physical Education and Recreation Journal*, (November/December) 41(2), pp. 11-13.

Orlick, T., Botterill, C. (1975) *Every Kid Can Win*. Chicago: Nelson-Hall. p. 12.

Petlichkoff, L. (1994/95) Introductory philosophy: developing the appropriate objectives in sport. *Coaching Focus*. 27, (Winter), pp. 3-4.

Powell, K., Thompson, P., Caspersen, C., Kendrick, J. (1987) Physical activity and the incidence of coronary heart disease. *Annual Review of Public Health*. 8, pp. 253-287.

Pridham, S., Hauswirth, M. (1992) *Success Stories*. Victoria: Sport Management Group. p. 3.

Roberts, G.C., Treasure, D. (1993) The importance of the study of children in sport: an overview. *Coaching Children in Sport*. London: E&FN SPON. pp. 3-16.

Rowland, T.W. (1990) *Exercise and Children's Health*. Champaign: Human Kinetics. p. 178.

Schreiber, L. (1990) *The Parents' Guide to Kids' Sports*. Boston: Little, Brown and Company.

Seefeldt, V., Ewing, M., Walk, S.E. (1992) *An overview of youth sports*. Washington DC: Paper commissioned by the Carnegie Council on Adolescence.

Shephard, R. (1984) Physical activity and wellness of the child. *Advances in Pediatric Sport Sciences*. 1, Champaign: Human Kinetics. pp. 1-30.

Spink, K. (1988) *Give Your Kids a Sporting Chance*. Toronto: Summerhill Press.

Todd, D. (1996) Sports: the games we play promote everyday values. *The Ottawa Citizen*. April 27th.

Part Two

Sport Participation

When should children specialize in sport? ▶

Malcolm Carmichael

Experts agree that in most cases, children should avoid specialization and work on developing a wide range of sport skills. Not until the child grows into adolescence should parents and coaches encourage specialization. If teenagers display skill and talent and love for a sport, increasing the amount of time spent training may be appropriate.

Lyle Sanderson, associate professor of physical education at the University of Saskatchewan, says prepubescent children should be encouraged to play as many sports as they can to develop a wide range of motor abilities.

Children, from approximately eight years of age until the onset of puberty, need to be placed in sports where they will receive competent instruction and work on developing sports skills. These are the 'skill-hungry years', when a child's ability to develop movement patterns is much higher than in adolescence. Specializing too early in sport means children will miss out on a broad base of activities.

"What's happening in gymnastics and swimming is absolutely criminal," says Sanderson. "Eight-year-old kids spending 20 hours or more in the gym are not being prepared for life."

Children who spend too much time involved in one particular sport may run the risk of burning out physically and emotionally. They may lack the well-rounded life experience that is needed to grow into emotionally healthy adults.

"I don't think being completely focused in any one area is ever good for a child," says Sanderson. "If you lose the ability to play that sport, you may think that you've lost everything."

Children need free time just to play, says Sanderson. Many parents who want the best for their children put them into too many organized activities. "It's just as healthy to let kids kick a ball around or play hide-and-seek."

Children should be exposed to as many different activities during the skill-hungry years. Before the adolescent growth spurt, children have a great capacity to develop the rough form of motor skills. Early specialization limits a child's potential in all sports, including the one in which he or she is currently specializing.

What are the risks of early specialization? ▶

any parents dream that their child will be the next Wayne Gretzky or will win an Olympic medal like Silken Laumann.

Such dreams have their price. Becoming a champion can require as much as 10 years or more of intensive preparation. Even then, success is never guaranteed. For the child, the rewards may be non-existent — a lost childhood, a damaged psyche, a life plagued by injuries, or the taint of athletic failure. Children who specialize in sport and experience a great deal of success at an early age may have difficulty coping with athletic failure later in life.

In *Little Girls in Pretty Boxes*, sportswriter Joan Ryan lifts the lid on what can happen in the process of shaping elite female gymnasts and figure skaters. She describes the training that drives young athletes to breaking point. Her book is a chronicle of eating disorders, stunted growth, stress fractures, and family break-ups. Ryan says the extraordinary demands of training can be compared to child abuse.

Leading children into early specialization has its cost. Swimmer's shoulder, tennis elbow, and runner's stress fracture are chronic overuse problems common with repetitive training cycles. Doctors are reporting a dramatic increase in the occurrence of these overuse injuries, even for younger children.

Physical education professor Lyle Sanderson says that many parents and coaches still believe that early specialization is the key to high performance. He reminds parents that not all children develop at the same rate, and that many young superstars may simply be maturing at an earlier chronological age than other children.

The role of parents and coaches is to help children make good decisions about their involvement in sport. Just as a loving parent guides a child away from a sweet treat before bedtime, he or she should encourage appropriate involvement in sport and a well-rounded, healthy lifestyle.

What are the signs of overtraining in sport?

O vertraining is a complex phenomenon, and the specific causes are not yet fully understood. Preventing this condition is difficult because the symptoms are highly individual and there are no clear warning signs. However, there is general concensus that once overtraining has been diagnosed, prolonged rest is the only cure.

Symptoms of overtraining may include lethargy, a loss of appetite, an increase in the incidence of infections, disturbed sleep patterns, and depression. The athlete will not perform at his or her usual level, may no longer want to compete, and may drop out of sport altogether.

Youth overtraining may also be the cause if a child
• is easily fatigued and irritated
• has physical complaints or eating problems
• loses self-esteem
• shows increased moodiness and/or self-criticism.[1]

Generally speaking, youngsters who suffer from overtraining experience persistent fatigue and their performance decreases. Being tired after exercise is normal, but when an athlete is constantly tired and lacks energy, overtraining may be the cause. Experts agree that rest and recovery after exercise is a critical component of every training program.

Overtraining is not common in youth sport, but it may surface in sports where younger children are engaged in formal regular training. Dr. Roy Shephard, professor emeritus of applied physiology at the University of Toronto's School of Physical and Health Education, says that on average, children will not push themselves to the point of over-exertion; however, it is possible for an over-enthusiastic coach to do this.

A child does not have to be an elite athlete to suffer from overtraining. Training that is either too frequent, too intense, too long, or does not include adequate rest can make athletes of all ages and abilities suffer from physical and mental fatigue.

When winning and high-level performance are over-emphasized, the danger of the child suffering negative effects increases greatly. The negative effects can come from the demands being too high in a single training session, but are more often the result of the child training too hard and too often over a long period of time. For instance, too much emphasis on breaking age group records can be a cause of overtraining in young athletes.

Does maturity affect performance?▶

Some youngsters start puberty very early or very late. There is no need for parents or coaches to overreact to this situation. Research shows that at age 12, there can be a four-year difference in the physical maturity of children. An early maturer can be a foot taller and weigh 30 or 40 pounds more than a late developer.

In sports such as hockey or basketball which require strength, power, and speed, the more mature child will usually perform better and fitness levels will be greater than in less developed peers. In certain sports, the opposite is true. Being big and tall is a disadvantage to a gymnast or a figure skater. The less a skater weighs, the easier it is to land jumps.

The uneven spread of early and late developers creates a difficult challenge. Many coaches with no understanding of this phenomenon choose certain kids to play on their teams for the wrong reasons. The early developers may have a lot of success in sport. They are picked first for team sports and receive much of the coach's attention. This may cause late bloomers to develop low self-esteem and many drop out of sport.

The most famous example of a late bloomer is basketball star Michael Jordan, who was cut from his junior varsity high school team and went on to become one of the greatest players of all time.

Lately, a concern about late bloomers has surfaced within ice hockey. It began with the NHL drafting 18-year-olds. Today, scouts are looking for even younger players. That means the NHL may miss out on late bloomers like Hall-of-Famers Guy Lapointe and Larry Robinson, both of whom began to skate at age 13.

Parents and coaches must encourage and nurture late developers to keep them in sport long enough to benefit from their eventual maturity. Towards the end of adolescence, late developers often surpass and become better athletes than early developers. Many of Canada's Olympic athletes have been late developers. Freestyle skier Lloyd Langlois soared through the air on his way to an Olympic medal, but as a child, he floundered on the ice in a town where everybody played hockey.

How much exercise do children need to stay fit?▶

In general, children need at least 30 minutes of vigorous physical activity every day. Each session should include a cardiovascular component to sufficiently increase a child's heart rate well above resting conditions. Even though most cardiovascular diseases are considered to be adult illnesses, fatty deposits have been detected in the arteries of children as young as three years of age, and high blood pressure exists in about five per cent of children. Aerobic exercise can make the heart pump more efficiently and reduces the risk of cardiovascular diseases.

Dr. Michel Portmann, a professor in the Département de Kinanthropologie, Université du Québec à Montréal, and coach of 1996 Olympic gold medallist Bruny Surin, says that children don't have to exercise diligently when they are young. Activities such as playing on monkey bars, running, and skipping every day will keep them fit. Parents and coaches can judge whether children are fit by watching them in play, noting their ability to move with energy. A child who tires easily or does not seem to have the energy needed to play actively may need more exercise.

Unfortunately, children are three to four times less active than they were 40 years ago. A recent study indicates that almost 40 per cent of five- to eight-year-old children in North America can be classified as obese. Obesity rates in Canadian children have increased by 50 per cent over the past 15 years. The 1988 *Campbell's Survey on Well-Being in Canada* reported that only 10 per cent of Canadian youth are active intensely enough to receive the health benefits associated with regular physical activity.

One cause of this phenomenon is the unacceptable decline in the physical education programs of most Canadian schools. The Canadian Institute of Child Health reports that the average Canadian child only takes physical education twice a week and a mere 12 per cent of children are receiving daily physical education. This decline in physical activity means that fewer children will enjoy the improved health that comes from daily exercise.

As children grow older, their lives become more sedentary. Many take the bus or are driven to school where they sit behind a desk all day. In the evening, they watch TV or play computer games. On average, the Canadian child and youth watches 26 hours of television per week. This is in addition to the 25 to 30 hours they spend sitting in school.

How does a school rate in terms of its physical education program? ▶

Louise Dickson

◀W ith declining school budgets, many of Canada's schools have dropped physical education programs from their course curriculum. Dr. Andrew Pipe, medical director of the Heart Check Centre at the University of Ottawa Heart Institute, said in a recent *Canadian Medical Association Journal* that Canada needs to shift its priorities. "This is a nation that exhorts 40-year-olds to 'participact' yet denies instruction in health and activity to its 14-year-olds."

A recent Gallup poll found that 85 per cent of Canadians surveyed favoured daily physical education as a required subject, starting in public school and running through high school. It's a position supported by the Canadian Medical Association, the Heart and Stroke Foundation, and the federal government through Fitness Canada. Yet only 18 per cent of Canadian schools have a plan in place to increase the amount of daily physical education they provide.

The Canadian Association for Health, Physical Education, Recreation and Dance (CAHPERD) has developed a physical education report card to help parents grade their child's school.

1. Does the school provide children with at least 30 minutes of instruction in physical education each day?
2. Does the program include participation in school intramural activities and student leadership opportunities?
3. Are a wide variety of physical activities offered?
4. Does the program include a cardiovascular component with activities such as running, skipping, aerobic dance, or swimming?
5. Does the program encourage children of all body types and abilities to participate?
6. Does the program emphasize fun, socialization, and active living rather than just competition and traditional team sports?
7. Are the teachers qualified?
8. Does the school provide a safe learning environment for physical activity?
9. Does the school make use of other facilities in addition to a gymnasium such as a school skating rink or community pool?
10. Does your child look forward to physical education classes and intramural activities?

If all 10 answers are "yes", your child's school has an excellent program. If you have between 6 and 8 "yes" answers, the program is good. If you have fewer than 6 "yes" answers, find ways to implement better programs.

Should co-ed participation be encouraged?

T here is no proven safety reason to prevent boys and girls from participating together in most sports up to approximately 11 years of age, or the beginning of the adolescent growth spurt.

Research shows there are no physical or psychological reasons to separate boys from girls in the years before puberty. Although boys generally are taller and weigh more than girls, the differences are small and they do not make much difference in sport. Boys are stronger, but girls, on average, are more flexible.

Sport is a great way for boys and girls to develop a healthy respect for each other from a very early age. Breaking down barriers on the playing field may prevent inequality later in life.

However, many young girls do not enjoy co-ed participation because of the difference in skill level and aggression between boys and girls. Some talented and early maturing girls can enjoy and benefit from co-ed participation. But many girls find that they do not receive enough attention from other players or the coach, there is too much emphasis on competition, or the boys tend to tease or bully them. These girls would be much better served in a girls-only environment.

According to the Canadian Association for the Advancement of Women and Sport and Physical Activity (CAAWS), playing on a girls' team that has the same opportunities as a boys' team is the best situation for girls and for increasing the numbers of girls in sport. CAAWS reports that boys still receive more resources, a wider choice of activities, and more competitive opportunities than girls. Until such time as the sport system is equitable, a girl's choice to try out and play on a boy's team should be supported. Sport organizers should continue to work towards increasing the opportunities for girls in sport by providing more girls' teams and leagues.

Is competitive sport too stressful for children? ▶

◄**C** ompetitive sport may be too stressful if a child is made to feel that self-worth depends on how he or she plays. When the things most important to children — such as love and approval — are made contingent on playing well, they are likely to experience great stress. Research shows that the fear of failure and a child's concern about not performing well may be the main sources of stress and anxiety in children's sport.

Children worry that they will fail, that they will not be able to live up to the demands of competition. Children can feel competitive stress before, during, and after competitions. One U.S. study showed that 62 per cent of youths worried about not playing well and about making a mistake, and 23 per cent said anxiety could prevent them from playing in the future.

Children who take part in individual sports may feel more competitive stress than those who play team sports. And pre-competition anxiety is greatly increased when parents pressure their children to win. The uncertainty surrounding a competition, how important the competition is, or how soon a child will compete can also add to the level of stress.

Sport psychologist Dr. Rainer Martens, an expert on children's sport, suggests that "competitive stress may be likened to a virus. A heavy dose all at once can make a child ill. A small dose carefully regulated permits the child to learn how to channel anxiety so that it aids rather than inhibits performance. Carefully selected competitions together with realistic objectives and expectations will enable the child to learn that sport is fun and can be enjoyed whatever the result."[2]

There is some concern that the stress in competitive sport may hinder the emotional development of young children. Some experts question whether young children should be involved in organized training and competition at all. They suggest that children are not old enough to cope with the anxieties that are integral to competitive sport. However, research conducted by Dr. Martens and Dr. Julie Simon showed that although sport does cause stress, it is no worse than that experienced when taking an academic test or performing in the school band.

What are the
signs of
competitive
stress? ▶

Some children are more naturally prone to anxiety and stress than others. The term 'trait anxiety' has been developed to describe these individuals. Children high in trait anxiety tend to view the world as more threatening than do children with low trait anxiety. Such children, often described by their parents as 'worriers', may find competitive sport more stressful than do others. Children with poor self-confidence and low self-worth, who feel they have little control over situations, may also experience more stress.

Parents and coaches can watch for signs that identify children who are particularly prone to stress and who may not be coping well with pressure. Stress can range from 'butterflies in the stomach', to extreme fear and panic, to avoidance of a competition or performance altogether. Loss of concentration, worry, rapid heart rate, nausea, stomach ache, fidgeting, restlessness, and fatigue are all signs of stress.[3]

Stress also causes muscle tension. Prolonged muscle tension leads to pain, stiffness, and fatigue. Children who are under stress will tire more easily, find it more difficult to make decisions, become forgetful, and lose concentration.

Other common signs and symptoms associated with childhood anxiety are
- loss of sleep, early waking, or any change in sleep patterns
- nightmares or bad dreams
- any change in dietary habits such as loss of appetite
- mood changes such as irritability or aggression
- manipulativeness — the child may become very controlling of situations
- restlessness or fidgeting
- hypochondriasis — the child may complain of physical symptoms on the day of the competition
- frequent urination or diarrhea.[4]

To gauge the level of stress, find out how the child feels before a competition. Parents can ask a child if he or she feels uptight or queasy or is worrying about making a mistake. Giving lots of positive reinforcement each time a child participates in a competition or performs a sport skill will avoid placing an undue emphasis on mistakes.

Are some children better able to cope with stress than others?▶

N o two children are exactly alike in the way they cope with stress, and some are able to cope better than others. Experts now believe that several factors influence a child's ability to cope with stress with a child's personality, intelligence, and self-esteem all playing a role.

In an article in *Coaching Children in Sport* entitled "Causes of Children's Anxiety in Sport," Stephen Rowley writes that factors such as the gender of the child, the child's intelligence, and the support from parents and coaches may influence a child's ability to cope with stressful situations. He made the following points:

- Unlike the pattern after adolescence, before puberty boys are more prone to competitive anxiety than girls. The reason for this difference may be that parents are less supportive of boys who can't cope with stress, or the importance of sport may be greater for boys.

- There is some evidence to suggest that children who are clever in school may be better able to cope with stress. It may be that these children have higher self-esteem or better problem-solving skills than their peers.

- The presence of close, supportive relationships with family, friends, or the coach plays an important part in protecting a child from stress. If children feel they can talk about their worries and anxieties, the symptoms of stress decrease significantly.[5]

Recognizing the influence that adults have on children and how stressful they perceive a sport competition to be is critical to understanding some of the many sources of competitive stress. In *Sport for Children and Youths*, Dr. Tara Scanlan writes, "Sport is a public affair. In contrast to the achievement in the classroom where passing or failing a math test can be an unobserved private experience, a hit or a strike is witnessed by teammates, opponents, coaches, parents, and spectators."[6]

Young children who feel pressure from parents and coaches to perform well or to win a competition will experience greater precompetition stress.

"To win the game and lose the child is totally an unworthy sacrifice."
Dr. Terry Orlick, Dr. Cal Botterill
Every Kid Can Win

At what age should children become involved in competitive sport?

Dave O'Malley

C hildren tend to be attracted to competitive sport. From an early age, they try to jump higher, throw further, or climb higher than their brothers and sisters. Competition is not a problem for young children. Problems only arise when someone else — usually a poorly-informed coach or an overly-enthusiastic parent — distorts competition by over-emphasizing the value of winning.

The Coaching Association of Canada recommends that children can begin to participate in suitably designed competitive sport after the age of about 11. However, children learn better in a non-stressful environment. Young children under the age of 11 are still trying to develop their capabilities. Excessive stress could lead to low self-image and will severely hinder this learning process.

David Carmichael is director of research and development at the Ontario Physical and Health Education Association in Toronto. He says children should begin their sporting experience in a child-centred program appropriate to their level of development. Opportunities should be provided for all children to play at their own level, including the late bloomer, the more sensitive, or the clumsy child.

Sport psychologist Dr. Terry Orlick has long been advocating the benefits of a joyful and cooperative sport environment. His book, *The Cooperative Sports and Games Book*, suggests how games can be altered to adopt a cooperative play approach.

Many of Canada's national sport organizations have also recognized the benefits of cooperative play and have adapted their programs to meet the needs of young players. For example, the Canadian Hockey Association developed the Initiation Program for children under the age of eight. This program replaces the competitive element in hockey with an emphasis on teaching young players the basic fundamentals of the sport, fair play, and fun.

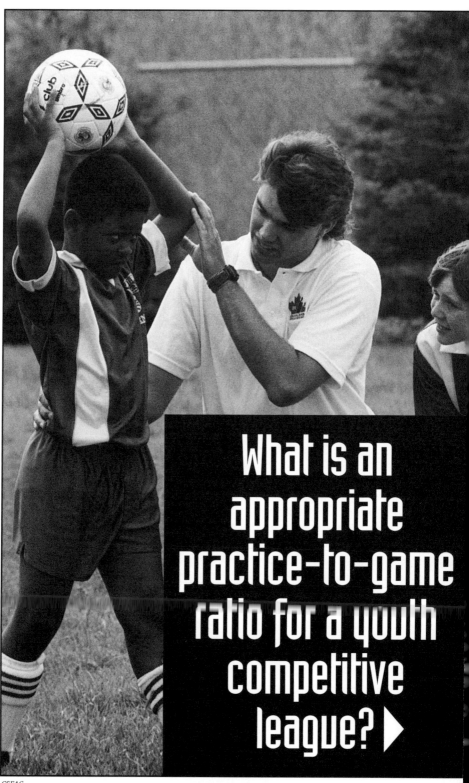

What is an appropriate practice-to-game ratio for a youth competitive league? ▶

I deally, children between the ages of six and 12 years should attend three to four practices for each game they play.

In reality, the opposite seems to be true. Sports columnist Roy MacGregor says, "In hockey, research shows that kids are being exposed to about three games to every practice. Parents are putting tremendous pressure on coaches to organize games because they want to see their kids score not skate."

Dr. Vern Seefeldt, director emeritus of the Institute for the Study of Youth Sports at Michigan State University, says, "When children get involved in an adult model of a game, the emphasis on skill development is reduced in lieu of the team's desire to win. Coaches tend to play those who are most likely to score and the more skilled players tend to dominate the game."

Many competitive leagues have extensive game schedules and maintain league standing records which culminate in post-season playoffs and a championship. House leagues which provide organized, structured competitions usually have equal playing time for all players regardless of ability and do not publish league standings. All teams make the playoffs. However, house leagues have limited practice times.

The tremendous growth in the importance of professional sport has spilled over into youth sport. More emphasis is being placed on children to compete more often and at a higher level. Competitive leagues, even at the youth level, try to model the professional ranks and organize youngsters into rigorous competitive schedules.

Professional hockey players in the NHL typically play an 80+ game season," says consultant Tim Robinson of the Coaching Association of Canada. "Some competitive leagues are trying to match this schedule for young children. This heavy competitive schedule makes it nearly impossible for young kids to learn new skills. Children involved in a competitive league should have a minimum of three sessions per week, two of which are designed to work on skill development."

Former coach Ken Shields, now president of the Commonwealth Centre for Sport Development in Victoria, notes that parents who have assumed the role of coach find it much easier to organize a game than to plan and implement a practice featuring effective skill development. "Much of our sport system relies on volunteer coaches, many of whom do not have expertise in the systematic design of skill learning. We need to help them in this regard. Remember, it takes years for teachers to understand the process of learning in young kids and to perfect the art of teaching skill progressions."

Should young children be involved in off-season training?

Lorraine Hendry

In general, the answer is "no." Young children under the age of about 11 should be experiencing a wide variety of different sport activities and should not focus their efforts exclusively on one sport.

Superstar Wayne Gretzky's dad, Walter, agrees. Wayne didn't play hockey in the summer. "I wouldn't allow him to play in the off-season," Walter Gretzky says. "He was encouraged to play other sports and get involved in other activities."

Depending on the sport, off-season training is unrealistic for young children. "The hockey season typically runs from September to April," says coaching consultant Tim Robinson. "I don't encourage my kids to participate in summer hockey programs. If they did, they would miss the opportunity to play summer sports such as baseball, tennis, and swimming. The skills they learn through participation in these sports will help them with all their motor skills in the long run."

Summer hockey is now said to be contributing to the dropout rate in ice hockey by burning out 13-year-olds. Former Calgary Flames coach Dave King believes that requiring children to commit to hockey alone is a mistake. "There's a lot to be said for playing more than one sport. Soccer, for example, develops agility and quick feet. These skills are very useful for hockey players."

On the other hand, some sports, tennis for example, have a short competitive season, generally running from June to September. It may not be unreasonable to register a child for a set of indoor tennis lessons during the winter if he or she is interested.

The 10 most important reasons I play my best school sport.

1. To have fun.

2. To improve my skills.

3. To stay in shape.

4. To do something I'm good at.

5. For the excitement of competition.

6. To get exercise.

7. To play as part of a team.

8. For the challenge of competition.

9. To learn new skills.

10. To win.

Sample: 2,000 boys and 1,900 girls, grades seven to 12, who identified a "best" school sport. From the 1987 study on youth sport conducted by Dr. Martha Ewing and Dr. Vern Seefeldt.

Are there special benefits for girls participating in sport?▶

There are several unique benefits for girls who participate in sport. In the past, school was the main place where girls could be successful. Sport offers a wonderful opportunity for girls to be successful outside the classroom as they experience new challenges and learn new skills.

Sport also helps girls break down the traditional female myths linking accomplishments to looks and beauty. It gives young girls a better appreciation of their bodies and they may be less likely to smoke and be pressured by the razor-thin images of females typical of the advertising media and the fashion industry. Although some sports such as gymnastics and figure skating are frequently linked with eating disorders in young girls, most sports give young girls a healthy attitude about their bodies.

Health professionals now recognize that girls, who tend to smoke more than boys, use smoking as a means of weight control. Dr. Carole Guzman, former president of the Canadian Medical Association, reports that among young people, high levels of fitness are associated with a lower level of smoking and drinking behaviour, healthier eating habits, and with increased self-esteem.

A recent University of Southern California study reports that a young women's risk of developing breast cancer is significantly reduced if she engages in regular physical exercise as early in life as her first menstrual period.

Are some children better suited to individual or to team sports?

It is hard for parents to know whether a child will be a team player or take to individual sports. And there's no research to prove certain temperaments make better individual athletes or produce stronger team members.

Experts agree that giving children an opportunity to participate in both individual and team sports will help them to make the choice that's right for them. Children will eventually show their preference by saying they prefer skiing to soccer or hockey instead of swimming.

Young girls, in particular, should be encouraged to participate in both individual and team sports. Girls typically lean towards individual sports. That means they miss out on the lessons learned in a team environment such as how to be a leader and how to be a team player.

If children are having trouble at school, should they be permitted to participate in sport? ▶

I n general, children should be encouraged to continue their sport involvement because all children need exercise as part of their day. Without physical activity, many have difficulty concentrating on their school work. In fact, studies have shown that active children tend to do better in school. A six-year study conducted in Québec found that youngsters who received five extra hours of physical activity per week achieved higher marks in academic subjects than students in regular programs.

The Canadian Association of Principals states that children who engage in physical education on a daily basis come to class ready to learn. They play better with others, have less aggressive behaviours, and display improved individual and class behaviour.

Furthermore, children who have difficulty with school work can use a boost in self-esteem which sport often provides. As they develop a sense of accomplishment in sport, this increase in self-confidence can often carry over into school. However, if practices and other sports-related demands are excessive, talk to the coach about the child's need to devote adequate time to studies.

"According to a Gallup poll, 94 per cent of Canadians believe physical education is as important as mathematics and reading."

Should children be allowed to quit a sport?

Early in life, children should be encouraged to try many sports. In some cases, quitting a sport may become a sensible option. Sometimes a child loses interest in a sport and participation may become a negative experience. Often a child realizes a sport does not suit his or her abilities and interests.

Find out the reasons why the child wants to quit. Although you may not want a child to make a habit of it, dropping out may be acceptable.

When is it appropriate to adapt sport for children? ▶

C hildren should not be playing adult sport, says former national level soccer coach Dr. Stuart Robbins. The rules of the game and the strategies are based on the ability of adults to socialize, work together, and compete against others. The equipment and size of the playing area are designed to challenge adult bodies.

Equipment has to be the right size for young players. Bats and racquets that are too heavy make it harder for children to develop basic physical skills, and they end up using the wrong techniques.

Children need to use equipment safely and successfully. Because it is hard for them to hit a ball, bats and racquets should have a proportionately larger striking surface. Balls should not be too fast or too hard.

If sport is adapted to meet the mental and physical needs of young players, they'll have more fun, they'll play more often, and they'll become more skillful.

Chances are, if children play eight-a-side soccer, they'll be running more and kicking the ball more often than if there are 11 players on each team. Playing six-a-side, with small goals and a suitably sized ball makes even more sense, says Dr. Robbins.

Even with the fairest hockey coach in the world, most children spend two-thirds of a game sitting on the bench. But if the ice is divided into three, there can be three six-a-side games played simultaneously with all the kids playing all the time. Similarly, children will develop volleyball and basketball skills much more quickly if they play three-a-side.

"Pure Joy"

Sport psychologist Dr. Terry Orlick, author of *Feeling Great*, says children love to play. It's the centre of their life. He recalls a group of young cyclists emerging from a mountain bike trail, covered in mud from head to toe and laughing happily. They had gone through every puddle they could find. "Just like the toddler who wants to jump in every puddle on the street, these kids had a blast on their bikes. They had great exercise, great challenge, and going through those puddles was part of the pure joy of the experience."

Should children with an underlying medical condition get involved in sport?

Absolutely, says Dr. Kathryn Keely, Canadian representative to the Committee on Sports Medicine and Fitness of the American Academy of Pediatrics. Doctors, parents, and coaches can work together to prepare children with chronic medical conditions to play sports safely.

The most important factor in involving a child with a medical condition in sport is that the appropriate people know about the specific problem and medical history and how to deal with it. Children should be taught to tell the coach if they are not feeling well. Coaches and teachers must be aware of the condition and have an emergency plan if the child runs into trouble.

Some children with asthma, for example, have no trouble exercising. But many must use caution because exercise is a known trigger of an asthmatic attack.

If a coach doesn't know a child has asthma, he or she might send the youngster charging off full-steam at the beginning of a practice. When the child begins to cough and wheeze and run out of energy, the coach might assume that he or she is out of shape. Instead, an asthmatic attack is occurring and the child needs medication to open up the airways again. The child will most likely have an inhaler on hand.

Exercise-induced asthma usually happens after intense activity. When coaches are aware of the condition, they can plan an appropriate warm-up which may prevent an attack.

Just as children with asthma may improve their health with exercise, daily exercise is absolutely essential for children with diabetes. Parents must make sure that the child is eating properly, knows how to monitor sugar levels, and learns how to recognize symptoms.

If your child has a medical problem, ask your doctor what sports are appropriate.

Which sports suit children with a medical condition? ▶

T he benefits of exercise are the same for everybody. The sense of well-being and improved health and fitness that comes from exercise enriches the life of every child. That is why children with an underlying medical condition need to exercise.

Being active keeps the body fit and healthy. For children with a progressive disease such as cystic fibrosis, exercise may reduce some of the symptoms as the disease progresses. Increasing the strength of their respiratory muscles can make their disease less of a problem for a while.

Similarly, a child with muscular dystrophy who performs strength and endurance exercises may improve his or her quality of life. Swimming improves the flexibility of a child with cerebral palsy. Obese children can shed excess weight by increasing their activity level.

Parents whose children have a progressive disease have to understand the normal progression of the disease to know the capabilities of their children. As the disease changes, so will their tolerance to exercise. Parents must tailor the program to the needs and abilities of the child and understand the normal progression of the medical condition.

Parents must choose a sport or activity wisely if their child has a chronic medical condition such as asthma. Because the cold air of a hockey arena may trigger an asthmatic attack, parents may guide that child to the warm, humid atmosphere of a pool. Parents who do not want to discourage haemophiliac children from exercising can steer them away from contact sports towards volleyball, badminton, or swimming.

> *"Success at anything comes*
> *from a passionate desire to be*
> *the best you can be."*
>
> Tim Frick
> *Canadian women's wheelchair basketball coach*
> *Success Stories*

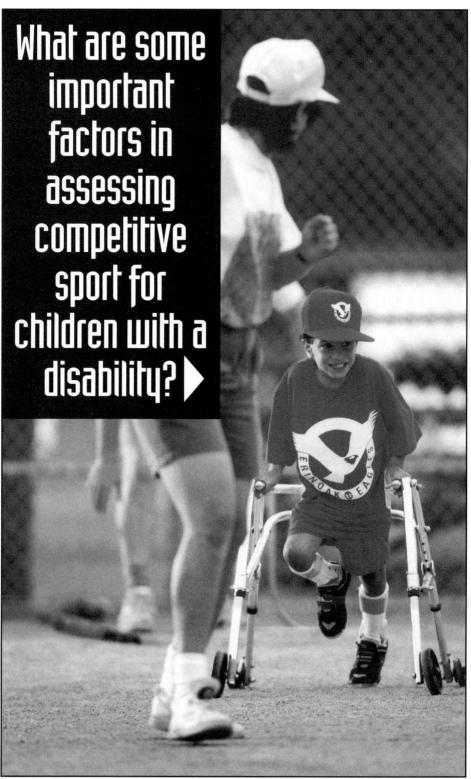

What are some important factors in assessing competitive sport for children with a disability? ▶

Peter J. Thompson

At every level, real competition means players compete against others of the same ability.

There are many sports and many levels of competition for people with a disability. The Paralympic Games represent the peak of disabled sports and are held shortly after the Olympic Games. Athletes who are Deaf have their own World Games. The Special Olympics are for individuals who are mentally challenged.

On a recreational level, activities can be adapted to allow a child to play sports with friends in the neighborhood. Sometimes it's a simple matter of tailoring an activity to meet the needs of a child with a disability. Sometimes, adapting is just not possible.

To choose an appropriate activity for a mentally-challenged child, parents must take into account the child's size, degree of coordination, health and fitness level, maturity, and motivation.

They need to ask: What are the child's cognitive abilities? What are the child's social skills? Will the child have trouble keeping up? Is there any risk in participating? Parents have to decide how active and competitive they want the activity to be. Because a child needs positive experiences, parents should have realistic expectations. A 12-year-old with the mental capacity of a four-year-old will not be able to concentrate at a two-hour practice.

Competitive sport for children with a disability must have enough competition to keep them interested, but not so much that they go away in tears. Parents and coaches should encourage children so that they want to come back. The rules of the game should be modified to suit the developmental level of the player.

"Athletes have to know you care, before they care what you know."

Jack Donohue
Former national men's basketball coach

Reference Notes

1 Marion, A. (1995) Overtraining and sport performance. *Coaches Report.* 2 (2), pp. 12-19.
2 Rowley, S. (1993) Causes of children's anxiety in sport. *Coaching Children in Sport.* London: E&FN SPON. p. 143.
3 Ibid., pp. 136.
4. Ibid., pp. 142.
5 Ibid., pp. 137-138.
6 Scanlan, T. (1986) Competitive stress in children. *Sport for Children and Youths.* Champaign: Human Kinetics. pp. 113

References

Armstrong, N., Balding, J., Gentle, P., and Kirby, B. (1990) Estimation of coronary risk factors in British schoolchildren: a preliminary report. *British Journal of Sports Medicine,* 24(1), pp. 61-66.

Benton, J. (1980) Sport specificity: The injury potential in our juvenile and adolescent athletes. *Arena Review.* 4, (December) pp. 12-15.

Bernstein, L. et al. (1994) Physical exercise and reduced risk of breast cancer in young women. *Journal of the National Cancer Institute.* 86(18). p. 1403.

Cahill, B., Pearl, A. (1993) *Intensive Participation in Children's Sports.* American Orthopedic Society for Sports Medicine. Champaign: Human Kinetics.

Canadian Association of Health, Physical Activity, Recreation and Dance. (1992) *Parents Information Kit.* Ottawa: Canadian Association of Health, Physical Activity, Recreation and Dance.

Campbell (1988) Campbell's Survey on Well-Being. In Fitness Directorate (Ed.) *Active Living and health benefits and opportunitie.* Ottawa: Canadian Association of Health, Physical Activity, Recreation and Dance.

Canadian Institute of Child Health (1995) Correspondence to Council of Ministers of Education. July 25th.

Carmichael, D. (1986) Focus on junior sport: what every adult should know about children and sport. *Sports Coach.* 10(3), pp. 41-45.

Chouinard, N., Trudel, P. (1993) A Report on the Structure and Organization of Novice Hockey in the Ottawa District Minor Hockey Association. Unpublished report. University of Ottawa.

Edwards, P. (1990) Fit kids finish first. *Canadian Living.* (September), pp. 127-129.

Elliot, L. (1980) Kids and stress. *Coaching Review.* 3(14) (March/April), pp. 37-40.

Fishburne, G., Harper-Tarr, D.A. (1990) An analysis of the typical elementary school timetable: a concern for health and fitness. *The Proceedings of the AIESEP World Convention,* July, London: E&FN SPON. pp. 362-375.

Forbes, W. (1987) (Producer) Flabby Kids. MIDDAY. Canadian Broadcasting Corporation.

Guzman, C.A. (1992) Related benefits from physical activity program interventions. In Fitness Directorate (Ed.) *Active Living and health benefits and opportunities.* Ottawa: Canadian Association of Health, Physical Education, Recreation and Dance.

Kingsbury, K. (1985) Inappropriate training: its symptoms and ill-effects. *Coaching Focus.* London: National Coaching Foundation. Autumn. 2, p. 4.

Kirkey, S. (1992) Kid couch potatoes. *The Ottawa Citizen.* July 24th.

Massimo, J. (1990) Coaching boys and girls. *International Gymnast.* (May) pp. 44-45.

MacGregor, R. (1993) Competitive madness. *The Ottawa Citizen.* November 20th.

National Coaching Certification Program. (1989) *Level 1 Theory.* Ottawa: Coaching Association of Canada.

National Coaching Foundation. (1989) *Working with Children.* Leeds: White Line Press.

Pierce, W.J., Stratton, P.K. (1981) Perceived sources of stress in youth sport participants. *Psychology and Motor Behavior and Sport.* 1980 North American Society for the Psychology of Sport and Physical Activity. Champaign: Human Kinetics. p. 11

Pipe, A. (1992) In S. Robbins (Ed.) *Canadian Medical Association Journal.* 146(5), pp. 763-765.

Pridham, S., Hauswirth, M. (1992) *Success Stories.* Victoria: Sport Management Group. p. 8.

Roberts, G.C., Treasure, D. (1993) The importance of the study of children in sport: an overview. *Coaching Children in Sport.* London: E&FN SPON. pp. 3-16.

Roberts, G.C. (1986) The perception of stress: a potential source and its development. *Sport for Children and Youths.* Champaign: Human Kinetics. pp. 119-126.

Rowley, S. (1993) Causes of children's anxiety in sport. *Coaching Children in Sport.* London: E&FN SPON.

Ryan, J. (1995) *Little Girls in Pretty Boxes: the making and breaking of elite gymnasts and figure skaters.* New York: Doubleday.

Scanlan, T., Passer, M.W. (1979) Sources of competitive stress in young female athletes. *Journal of Sports Psychology,* 1, pp. 151-159.

Scanlan, T. (1986) Competitive stress in children. *Sport for Children and Youths.* Champaign: Human Kinetics. pp. 113-118.

Scanlan, T. (1977) The effects of success-failure on the perception of threat in a competitive situation. *Research Quarterly.* 48, pp. 144-153.

Schor, E. (1995) *Caring for your School-Age Child. The American Academy of Pediatrics.* New York: Bantam Books.

Seefeldt, V., Ewing, M., Walk, S.E. (1992) *An overview of youth sports.* Washington DC: Paper commissioned by the Carnegie Council on Adolescence.

Shephard, R. (1982) *Physical Activity and Growth.* Chicago: Year Book Medical Publishers Inc.

Schreiber, L. (1990) *The Parents' Guide to Kids' Sports.* Boston: Little, Brown and Company.

Simon, J.A., Martens, R. (1979) Children's anxiety in sport and nonsport evaluative activities. *Journal of Sport Psychology.* 1, pp. 160-169.

Smith, R. (1986) A component analysis of athletic stress. *Sport for Children and Youths.* Champaign: Human Kinetics. pp. 107-111.

Smoll, F. (1986) Stress reduction strategies in youth sport. *Sport for Children and Youths.* Champaign: Human Kinetics. pp. 127-136.

Wilson, V.J. (1984) Help children deal with the stress factors found in competition. Momentum: *A Journal of Human Movemen Studies.* Edinburgh. 9(1), (Spring) pp. 26-28.

Part Three

How Children Grow And Develop

How do children grow and develop?▶

C ertain changes occur as children grow and develop. These changes — called stages of development — affect how a child performs in sport. The stages of physical and motor development influence how well a child performs sport skills. The stages of emotional development dictate what kind of competition is most suitable.

Motor development often does not proceed at the same rate as physical development. Rapidly growing children often appear awkward. The child may not be ready to execute or refine a skill until his or her motor ability develops further.

These stages of development are predictable and all children pass through them, says physical education professor Lyle Sanderson. However, the age at which the child enters each stage and the duration of each stage cannot be predicted. A youngster's developmental age can differ significantly from his or her chronological age by as much as two or more years in either direction.

PHYSICAL DEVELOPMENT
When children grow, they experience a change in hormone levels, in their muscles, bones and joints, their energy systems, and their cardiovascular systems (heart and lungs). Up to the onset of puberty, children grow at a steady pace, making regular gains in height and weight.

Coaches and parents must remember that there can be a wide variation in size among youngsters of the same age. In a typical elementary school classroom, height differences among children range from four to five inches.

Just as height can vary from one child to another, so can the timing of a child's growth. Despite the averages, many youngsters experience clear growth spurts, followed by periods during which they grow very little.

EMOTIONAL DEVELOPMENT
As the body grows, children also develop emotionally and intellectually. They gain a stronger understanding of themselves and the relationships they have in the adult world. They improve their ability to interpret, analyze, and think.

A very small child thinks of himself or herself as the centre of the world. Once children reach school age, they pay more attention to other people. As they get older, they are more capable of understanding team play and the relationships involved in team activity. A good coach recognizes the importance of social and mental development within sport by using team games, cooperative skills, and fair play as the basis of activity.

Are children naturally flexible? ▶

Not every child can bend and stretch like a rubber band. Some children, like some adults, are just not flexible. But if they train, children will gain flexibility faster than adults.

The muscle tissue in children is as flexible as muscle tissue in adults. What is quite different is the connective tissue. Children can extend their ligaments and tendons farther than adults can, says Dr. Keith Russell, associate professor of physical education at the University of Saskatchewan. "What boggles my mind is how stiff some young athletes are. Coaches aren't spending enough time stretching these kids. It's the best time of their life to do it. You can get such good results with such little effort."

It is particularly important for children to work on flexibility as they head toward their growth spurt. During rapid growth, flexibility decreases. If a child is not naturally flexible, the best time to gain range is *before* the growth spurt. Increased flexibility may prevent injuries, and also improves an athlete's performance.

To improve flexibility, children should always perform a proper warm-up followed by stretching exercises. They should also stretch during their cool-down. Effective stretching can improve performance, but overstretching can be harmful to the body by reducing the stability of joints.

CSFAC

Do genetics play a role in how successful children will be in sport?▶

Studies have shown that a person's performance level and response to training are strongly influenced by genetics. They have shown that children inherit not only physical characteristics, but also psychological qualities such as competitiveness and motivation as well. Heredity is therefore very important in determining how good an athlete a child can be.

Studies of identical twins show that approximately 50 per cent of aerobic power and 70 per cent of endurance performance are fixed by heredity. Research conducted at Université Laval by world-renowned genetics expert Dr. Claude Bouchard indicates that an individual's response to training is also genetically determined. This means that some athletes will show greater potential for improvement than others as a result of training, regardless of their initial level of fitness or how hard they work.

If a child does not have the genetic makeup required to excel in a particular sport, it is unlikely that he or she can perform at the highest level. Although genetics play a key role in determining one's potential for performance, it is clear that proper training is also critical. In fact, it is through training and hard work that genetic potential in sport can be realized.

Genetics play a big part in our ultimate level of achievement in sport, but everyone can and should be encouraged to participate. All children can benefit from the life-long lessons sport can bring them, regardless of their level of performance. Eventually, if performance is important to the child, it may be advisable to consider directing him or her to sports where the probability of success is highest.

Jeux de Canada Games

How Children Grow And Develop

What are the risks of 'making weight' for young children?

Everyone has heard of the dangers of athletes using steroids to 'bulk up'. Parents should know that the risks of losing too much weight are just as real. The Coaching Association of Canada does not condone weight loss in children's sport.

Children who participate in esthetic sports such as diving, rhythmic gymnastics, and figure skating may be asked by an overzealous coach to diet to improve their performance. Girls may be encouraged to reduce their weight because wider hips and weight gain reduce a body's agility. Unfortunately, without adequate food and energy, performance suffers and other problems may occur.

Dieting to prevent normal weight gain and growth has long-term, harmful consequences for young girls, says pediatrician Kathryn Keely. Long-term weight loss can reduce the bone density of young girls, increasing the risk of stress fractures and osteoporosis. An overemphasis on dieting may lead to life-threatening eating disorders such as anorexia nervosa or bulimia. Very thin girls may not get their periods because they weigh too little.

Boys, trying to make a certain weight class in football or wrestling, will often attempt to lose weight very quickly. Trying to lose five pounds before the morning weigh-in, they run around in plastic garbage bags, eat laxatives, swallow diuretics, starve themselves, and restrict fluids. Such extreme behaviour can cause a dangerous fluid loss in the athlete resulting in dehydration and electrolyte imbalances. During exercise, particularly in hot and humid weather, the body temperature of a dehydrated athlete can rise to dangerous levels. A body that is dehydrated has a reduced ability to cool itself through sweating, leading to heat injuries. The overall result is impaired performance.

"It's like somebody having horrible stomach problems and going out to compete," says Dr. Keely. By dehydrating, the athlete has reduced agility, concentration, quickness, and ability to sustain high aerobic exercise.

Everyone is born with a genetic code that determines body type. It is possible to make some adjustments within a healthy range. But no normal-weight child should ever reduce his or her energy intake when growing.

Should coaches monitor the weight of pre-adolescent children? ▶

There is no medical reason why children should be subjected to weigh-ins by a coach if they look healthy and well-nourished. But if a parent or a coach is worried that a child is training too hard, becoming too thin, or feeling too much pressure, he or she should be weighed to make sure weight is appropriate for height.

In some sports, a pre-season weigh-in is necessary to group children according to their size and strength. Beyond that, children should be weighed once a year by their pediatrician or family doctor.

Weighing a child every day or every week doesn't benefit the young athlete. The purpose of weigh-ins is usually to keep the child's weight low. And coaches have no business trying to get healthy children to lose weight.

There are many published accounts of coaches verbally abusing young athletes to get them to lose weight. There's no need to weigh a healthy figure skater or gymnast. Forcing them to think about and focus on their weight could make them develop debilitating eating disorders such as anorexia nervosa and bulimia. Excessive weight loss may also be an indication of overtraining.

If your child is being weighed, find out why. Make sure the weigh-ins are conducted in a responsible atmosphere with no negative consequences or pressures to the child for any weight loss or gain. The child shouldn't feel any pressure because he or she is gaining weight. It is normal to gain weight as one grows.

"Recognize the power inherent in the position of coach."
Coaching Code of Ethics
Canadian Professional Coaches Association

Should children perform exercises aimed at developing strength?▶

Strength training refers to all the exercises and activities that develop strength and power. Until recently, strength training in prepubescent children was discouraged because it was thought to be ineffective and dangerous.

Today, new research shows that it is possible for pre-adolescents to increase strength with little risk of injury in properly supervised programs. In fact, by strengthening muscles that cross a joint, strength training may even offer some protection to the child already participating in sports such as athletics, alpine skiing, ice hockey, and figure skating which require bursts of power and impose a lot of stress on young muscles and bones.

One of the main benefits of a well-designed strength program is that it balances the strength of muscle pairs. This balance is an important aspect of injury prevention. Alpine skiers, for example, typically have very strong quadriceps and need to strengthen their hamstrings to prevent knee injuries.

For children, strength training should be seen as only one of the many components of fitness. Alain Marion, a consultant with the Coaching Association of Canada, recommends that before resorting to weights, children should be directed to use body weight as the basis of strength training. This allows a more natural strength-building progression. Calf raises, push-ups, and chin-ups are all examples of strength-training methods using body weight.

Strength-training programs for pre-adolescent children must focus on low weights and relatively high repetitions. Heavy lifting and excessive repetitions must be avoided. A child should be able to perform 12 or 15 repetitions of each exercise when using resistance training equipment. If he or she can only lift a weight three to five times, it is far too heavy. Attempting to lift heavy weights is not an appropriate activity for children.

Without the supervision of a qualified instructor, children who lift weights can injure themselves. On their own, children may try to lift weights that are too heavy for them. A recent American survey showed that most injuries associated with strength training in children are the result of accidents in the home, as unsupervised youngsters attempt to lift heavy weights.

For athletes who are beginning to train with weights, it is also important to first learn sound lifting techniques. This can only be done using relatively light weights. In general, the emphasis should be on technique for approximately one year after the adolescent growth spurt.

Different People Need Different Amounts of Food

The amount of food you need every day from the 4 food groups and ot foods depends on your age, body size, activity level, whether you are r female and if you are pregnant or breast-feeding. That's why the Food gives a lower and higher number of servings for each food group. For example, young children can choose the lower number of servings, wh male teenagers can go to the higher number. Most other people can ch servings somewhere in between.

Grain Products
5-12
SERVINGS PER DAY

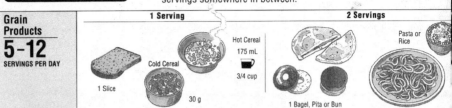

1 Serving

1 Slice

Cold Cereal

30 g

Hot Cereal
175 mL

3/4 cup

2 Servings

1 Bagel, Pita or Bun

Pasta or Rice

Vegetables & Fruit
5-10
SERVINGS PER DAY

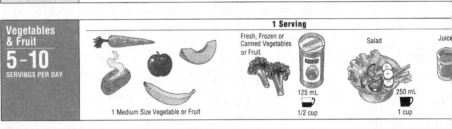

1 Serving

1 Medium Size Vegetable or Fruit

Fresh, Frozen or Canned Vegetables or Fruit

125 mL
1/2 cup

Salad

250 mL
1 cup

Juic

Milk Products
SERVINGS PER DAY
Children 4-9 years: 2-3
Youth 10-16 years: 3-4
Adults: 2-4
Pregnant & Breast-feeding
Women: 3-4

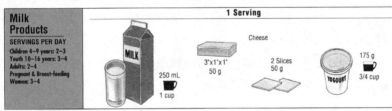

1 Serving

MILK

250 mL
1 cup

Cheese

3"x1"x1"
50 g

2 Slices
50 g

YOGOURT

175 g

3/4 cup

Meat & Alternatives
2-3
SERVINGS PER DAY

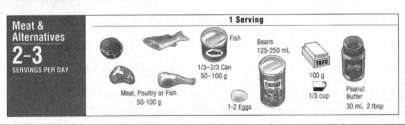

1 Serving

Meat, Poultry or Fish
50-100 g

1-2 Eggs

Fish
1/3-2/3 Can
50-100 g

Beans
125-250 mL

TOFU
100 g
1/3 cup

Peanut Butter
30 mL 2 tbsp

Other Foods

Taste an ment car come fro foods an ages tha not part 4 food g Some of foods ar in fat or so use t foods in modera

What are the nutritional requirements of young athletes? ▶

According to *Canada's Food Guide to Healthy Eating* every child needs a balanced diet with food chosen from the four main food groups — grain products, vegetables and fruit, milk products, and meat and alternatives. Healthy eating habits include a diet that is high in carbohydrates (55-60 per cent) and low in fat (no more than 30 per cent) and protein (12-15 per cent).

Marilyn Booth, sports nutrition program director with the Sport Medicine and Science Council of Canada, says that young athletes should eat a meal at least three hours before a game or practice so the stomach is not full by playing time. For pre-game nutrition, she advises parents and coaches to offer mainly carbohydrates such as cereals, breads, rice, pasta, potatoes, fruit, and vegetables, which are easy to digest and convert to energy.

The pre-game meal should also contain some protein and be low in fat because these foods are slower to digest. Protein-rich foods include meat, fish, poultry, eggs, dried beans, milk, yogurt, peanut butter, lower-fat cheese, and nuts. Fatty foods such as fried foods, bacon, sausages, fast-food burgers, sour cream, and salad dressings should be avoided.

Children should be encouraged to eat three healthy meals a day, regardless of their participation in sport. However, after activity, children need to replace fluids and their energy stores with juice and a snack. Fruit juice, bagels, and yogurt are examples of easy-to-carry snack foods to aid recovery after an activity.

According to the National Institute of Nutrition, the demands of growing combined with the physical stress of training and competition mean some young athletes may be undernourished. Depending on the type and intensity of exercise, they need more calories, more water, more protein, and more iron than inactive children. Iron deficiency can be a problem for athletes, particularly for girls who have begun to menstruate.

Food supplements, however, are unnecessary. If children are eating a good variety of foods from the four food groups, they are getting all the vitamins and minerals they need. Making a variety of healthy food choices available to children three times a day will instill good eating habits for life.

Growing children also need some fat in their diet as a concentrated energy source to keep up with growth spurts. During fast-growth periods, children should be able to eat as much as they want when they are hungry. If children learn to balance an active lifestyle with energy from a variety of foods, their long-term health will benefit.

How much water should children drink during exercise?▶

Τ he human body needs fluid to function. During exercise, children and adults lose body fluids, primarily through sweat. This water must be replaced to avoid dehydration. Oded Bar-Or, a research physician at McMaster University in Hamilton, Ont., says most people underestimate how much fluid they need to replace. How thirsty you are doesn't tell you how much you need to drink.

When fluids are not replaced during exercise, body temperature starts to rise. And because body temperature rises faster in children than in adults, young athletes must drink enough fluid to prevent dehydration.

Children need to drink every 15 or 20 minutes when they are exercising or even just playing in the playground, says Bar-Or. If it is hot and humid, children should go to the sidelines regularly to take a few sips of cool water. On each of these occasions, they should drink until they are no longer thirsty. Then, if they are under 10 years of age, encourage children to drink another half-cup. If older than 10 years of age, children should drink another cup.

The amount of fluid each child needs depends on body size, how hot and humid it is, and how hard he or she is exercising. "Teaching children to drink beyond thirst will prevent dehydration. Because physical activity suppresses the thirst mechanism, children need to be reminded to drink frequently," says Bar-Or.

You can tell if a child is dehydrated by checking the color of the urine. If the urine is dark and there is little of it, the child needs to replace lost fluids. Giving them a little too much water won't harm them, says Bar-Or. It will only make them go to the bathroom.

Studies conducted in Bar-Or's laboratory show that children will drink 45 per cent more water if it is flavoured. He suggests that parents flavour the water if it means children will drink more. Be sure that any flavouring added to the water low in sugar and salt content.

If fruit juice is consumed during activity, it should be diluted with water. Most juice has too much sugar and will not be absorbed very effectively unless it is diluted. A mixture of two or three parts water to one part juice has been found to be effective.

Are children more prone to heat and cold stress than adults?▶

Yes, children are more sensitive to heat and cold stress than adults. Heat tolerance is directly affected by body size. Children are smaller and weigh less, but because they have a larger relative surface area than adults, their ability to tolerate either heat or cold stress is affected.

During exercise, most of the energy released from the body appears as heat. The more we exercise, the more heat we build. And the more heat we build, the more we have to get rid of it. The evaporation of sweat is the most effective way to get rid of body heat.

Pound for pound, children build up more heat than adults. For example, if an adult and a child are walking, the child is accumulating more heat. To make things even harder, children do not sweat as much as adults.

Paradoxically, in cold conditions, children lose heat faster than adults and are more vulnerable to over-cooling. Children are more susceptible to cold stress because of their relatively large surface-to-mass ratio. Children also lose heat rapidly in cool water. The smaller the child, the faster the heat loss.

Children also take longer to acclimatize to changes in hot and cold weather. An adult body will acclimatize to a heat wave in about a week to 10 days; a child's body will take about 10 to 14 days. Adults should be aware that while they may be coping well with heat or cold, the child may not yet be acclimatized or may not have the same tolerance.

References

Athletics Canada. (1995) *Run, Jump and Throw*. Gloucester: Athletics Canada.

Bar-Or, O. (1980) Climate and exercising the child—a review. *International Journal of Sports Medicine*. (1) pp. 53-65.

Bar-Or, O. (1989) *Advances in Pediatric Sport Sciences: Volume 3. Biological Issues*. Champaign: Human Kinetics.

Blimkie, C., Marion, A. (1995) Resistance training during preadolescence: issues, controversies, and recommendations. *Coaches Report*. l(4), pp. 10-14.

Bouchard, C. (1986) Genetics of aerobic power and capacity. In R.M. Malina & C. Bouchard (Eds.), *Sport and Human Genetics*. Champaign: Human Kinetics. pp. 58-88.

Cahill, B., Pearl, A. *Intensive Participation in Children's Sports*. American Orthopaedic Society for Sports Medicine. Champaign: Human Kinetics.

Canadian Professional Coaches Association. (1995). *Coaching Code of Ethics*. Ottawa: Canadian Professional Coaches Association. p. 5.

Carlson, J., Le Rossignol, P. (1989) The child exercising in the heat. *Sports Coach*. April-June. pp. 16-20.

Gerrard, D. Farquhar, S., (1994) *Children in Sport: A Resource for Parents, Teachers and Coaches*. New Zealand Federation of Sports Medicine and the Hillary Commission for Sport, Fitness and Leisure.

Drabik, J. (1996) *Children's Sports Training*. Vermont: Stadion Publishing Company Inc.

Humphrey, J.H. (1991) *An Overview of Childhood Fitness*. Springfield: Charles Thomas Publisher.

National Coaching Certification Program. (1989) *Level 1 Theory*. Gloucester: Coaching Association of Canada.

Poliquin, C. (1994) *Free Body Strength Training*. Gloucester: Coaching Association of Canada.

Rowland, T.W. (1990) *Exercise and Children's Health*. Champaign: Human Kinetics. pp. 79-80.

U.S. Consumer Product Safety Commission. (1987) National electronic injury surveillance system. Directorate for Epidemiology. Washington: National Injury Information Clearinghouse.

Part Four

The Mind Of A Child

How do children think and learn? ▶

T eaching children new sport skills is not easy. It requires knowing how children learn, how they pay attention, remember, and make decisions.

ᴛe human brain is like a computer. It receives information by using its senses, terprets the information, and then produces a response. When children see baseball travelling towards them, they must feel where their body is and cognize that to hit the ball, they must swing the bat at a particular time and ᴇeed. The results of the swing are stored in memory for the next time.

owever, learning sport skills does not simply involve learning how to swing bat or kick a ball. It also involves learning what to pay attention to. In a team ᴇort, many things compete for a child's attention: teammates, opponents, the ᴇll or puck, coaches, and parents. Parents or spectators who shout from the ᴇelines can create distractions for players, making it difficult for them to ᴇrform.

ᴇ play a team sport, children must pay attention to cues that are relevant and ᴇock out those that are not. It is easy for children to become overloaded with ᴇformation. Keeping practices simple by giving youngsters only one thing to ᴇork on at a time improves the learning process.

ᴇeryone has a limited amount of information that can be processed at any one ᴇe; the speed with which we can deal with the information is known as our ᴇformation processing capacity. As we grow and mature, our capacity to handle ᴇformation becomes more sophisticated. We can deal with more information at ᴇce, and more quickly.

ᴇ help them learn, coaches must try to reduce the information children have ᴇ deal with. Playing basketball, for example, requires the child to dribble the ᴇll and look for a teammate — two tasks that are difficult until one of them ᴇquires less attention. To help children cope, coaches should give them time to ᴇactise dribbling alone. Then they can practise dribbling past standing players ᴇ cones. When children know how to dribble, coaches can start introducing ᴇssing techniques. When dribbling is automatic, the game is easier to learn.

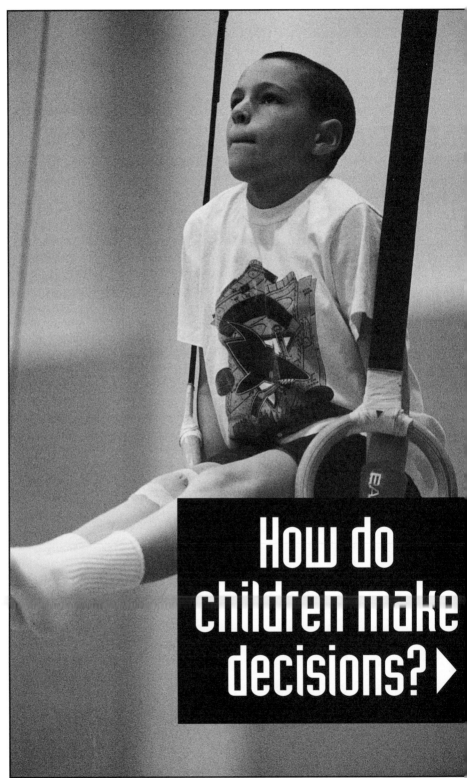

How do children make decisions? ▶

porting situations usually require quick and complex decision-making. Which pass should I use? With how much force? In which direction should I kick?

For children, making decisions in a new situation is a slow process. With their limited experience, they are much slower at making decisions than adults. And when their young minds are distracted by the stress or tension that comes with playing sport, it becomes even more difficult to make good decisions.

A child's capacity to learn new skills and to make decisions is limited by his or her capacity to process information. The more distractions children must cope with, the more difficult it is to learn. To enhance learning, a coach must free the child's attention from such distractions to make learning and decision-making easier.

To help children learn, coaches should adapt the sport for youngsters. Children are baffled by too many choices. A small group of players reduces the number of choices open to them and simplifies decision-making. Once children are confident, coaches can present more difficult situations which offer a larger number of possibilities. Therefore, three-a-side or four-a-side may be appropriate at the younger levels.

Coaches can also simplify the rules. Rules are normally written for games played at an adult level. Coaches should try to be flexible and think of rules as a framework that may need to be built upon slowly. Introduce rules as they are needed, and adapt them in order to focus on what you want the children to learn. Coaches can focus on a few simple, key words that allow for a gradual progression of skill learning.

Coaches can also teach children how to make decisions by creating a comfortable environment. A three-on-two practice drill requires easier decision-making than a two-on-two drill. Coaches must accept that making wrong decisions is part of the learning process. Teaching youngsters decision-making skills is a vital link to encouraging their self-reliance and making their experience enjoyable.

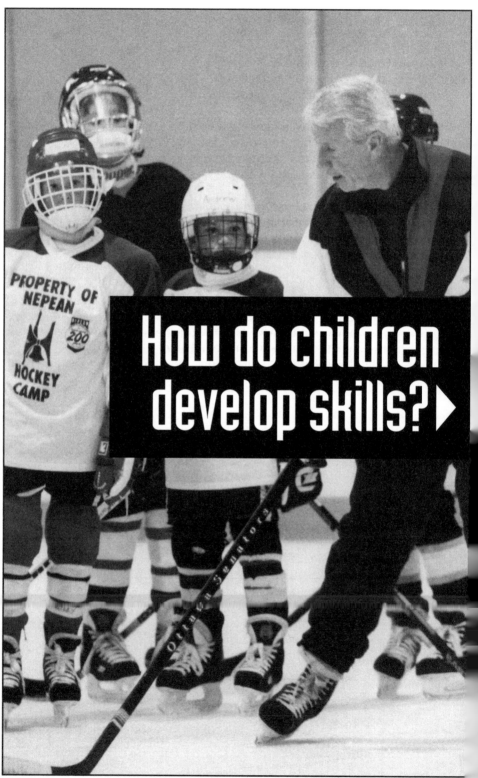

How do children develop skills?▶

W hen a baby learns to walk, it goes through a natural sequence of development — creeping, crawling, standing with support, then standing alone. Finally, it will walk, encouraged by delighted parents. The loving parent and the baby learning to walk is the best model to apply to children learning sport skills, says sport psychologist Dr. Murray Smith. A parent doesn't give walking lessons; he or she simply encourages the child.

Sport skills develop slowly from primitive to less primitive. Children rarely learn a new skill correctly at the start. Adults often make the mistake of trying to teach a child to throw, kick, or catch the ball the way they do. A coach who directs a child constantly is actually impeding the learning process. When children are learning, they make lots of mistakes. But they learn by thinking things through. When they detect an error, they are taking another step in skill development.

There are generally three stages to teaching children new skills: understanding, practising, and performing.

UNDERSTANDING
In the first stage, children must understand what they are trying to achieve. Never assume that children know what you want — show them, then explain in simple terms. Good coaches demonstrate the skill themselves and then ask several team members to try it. It is better to choose someone who can demonstrate the skill correctly at the athletes' present level. Most people identify with average performers and learn best from them. Beginners sometimes find it discouraging to observe the best performers.

PRACTISING
Once children understand what is to be achieved, practice is needed to refine the skills. Keep practices short, simple, and fun. During practice, give feedback that is appropriate to the age and skill level of the players. Children simply cannot absorb feedback as well as adults. Start by asking questions and deal with one thing at a time. Children learn more if they have to recall and think it through themselves. Always find something positive to say after each skill attempt and focus on key points.

PERFORMING
When a skill can be performed almost automatically, the child can then attempt it within a more complex or modified game situation.

Can children improve coordination through involvement in sport?

Dr. Geraldine Van Gyn, associate professor in kinesiology at the University of Victoria, says coordination is the capability to control the body's actions in time within our environment, with body parts moving in an appropriate manner. Just as an orchestra works together to make music, the body parts must move in the correct direction with the right amount of force and at the right time to create a coordinated action.

By about age six, most children are able to perform basic skills such as walking, running, hopping, jumping, throwing, and catching. More complex skills such as skipping will be a challenge, and many children look awkward or uncoordinated when they try them for the first time. In order for children to learn how to skip, they must link the actions of walking and hopping, using the correct timing. For most sport skills, timing is one of the most difficult tasks to learn. Imagine how difficult it is to learn how to catch a thrown or batted ball on the run: actions must be coordinated to catch the ball and move the body to the right place at the right time.

Coordination naturally develops with age, but greatly improves with experience and practice. If you want a child to be an ace pitcher or hitter, you have to spend time tossing the ball after school and on weekends. The average child can develop most skills with experience.

Van Gyn says that children who appear clumsy or uncoordinated when first learning a sport skill may be reluctant to continue their participation. "It is important that a child's initial experience be successful and positive so that he or she will be eager to participate further. With practice, coordination will improve." Some sports such as baseball, soccer, and swimming can be modified to accommodate young children learning new skills. T-ball is a good example of how to modify a sport.

Growth spurts which occur during puberty may affect coordination, warns Van Gyn. As the body's length and weight change, awkwardness and lack of coordination may result. But if the child continues to practise, this awkwardness will eventually disappear.

"The more time the child spends experiencing different kinds of sport and practising moving in different environments, the better coordination will become," says Van Gyn. Involvement in sport can help children to become coordinated movers, but sport involvement will only continue if the experience is positive.

Does sport help build self-esteem? ▶

R enowned child psychologist Jean Piaget believed that the most important phase in the development of self-esteem occurs between the ages of about six and 11. This is also a time when children are most likely to be introduced to sport. How children come to understand themselves and relate to others in social situations, such as sport, is essential in helping them develop mature social skills.

Research conducted in British Columbia with more than 650 parents found that the primary reason they register their youngsters in youth sport is to build self-esteem. And they're right. Success in sport will, in fact, help children build healthier self-esteem.

Very early in life, children begin to develop a picture of themselves, a self-image. They develop positive feelings about themselves and acquire a sense of importance and self-worth. The way in which they see and evaluate themselves — either positively or negatively — is known as self-esteem.

If children are given many opportunities to succeed in sport, they will more often come to see themselves as 'winners' rather than 'losers'. They will grow up to be better adjusted, more confident, and better able to cope with stress and new challenges.

A child's self-esteem is initially shaped by parents. Verbal and non-verbal reactions, praise and criticism, smiles, other facial expressions, and hugs help to influence a child's level of independence and sense of achievement. When children are given lots of praise and positive reinforcement, they develop high self-esteem.

Behavioural psychologist B.F. Skinner believes that personalities are shaped by the *positive* reinforcement received throughout a lifetime. According to Skinner, we are what we have been *rewarded* for being.

Sport provides children with opportunities to try new skills and assess their capabilities. As figures of authority, parents and coaches have an enormous capacity to make children feel good about themselves. Even casual remarks can have a great impact. Parents and coaches should always find something each child does well, even if it's just following directions, and give praise for that.

What are the building blocks to healthy self-esteem? ▶

nderstanding and support from parents are the main building blocks for feelings of self-worth. Parents should praise their children for learning and trying new things.

Sport psychologist Dr. Terry Orlick says that "helping youngsters develop high self-esteem is one of the most rewarding gifts that parents can give to children." Children need a healthy sense of self-esteem in order to feel good about themselves and good about others. Orlick's book, *Nice on My Feelings*, focuses on how self-esteem can be nurtured in young children and can help them believe in their own capacity.

Self-esteem is more than just a sense of happiness. It is an attitude of, 'I am capable; I can do this.'

"This kind of attitude develops when parents and coaches demonstrate a belief in children and encourage them to take responsibility for pursuing their own potential," says Orlick. A child with a high self-esteem is better able to cope with life's challenges, to pursue his or her potential, and to live joyfully.

"It is my responsibility to teach the athletes to be their own coaches."

Karen Strong
Former national women's cycling coach
Success Stories

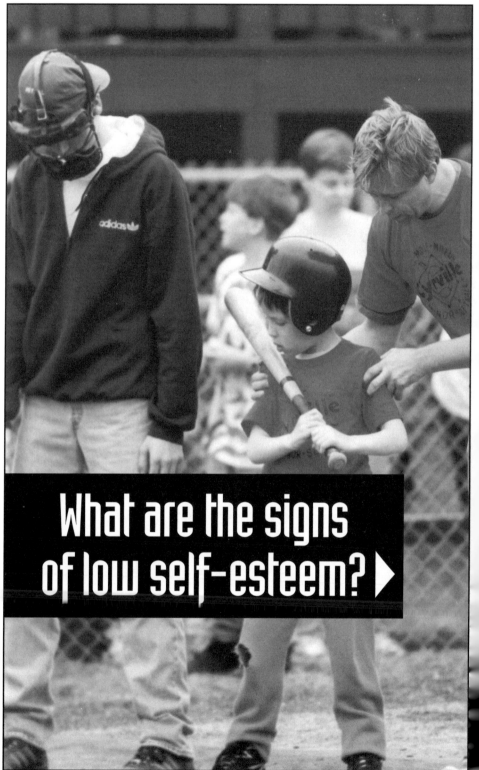

What are the signs of low self-esteem? ▶

T o help determine if a child has low self-esteem, the American Academy of Pediatrics recommends watching for the signals listed below. These signs could be everyday responses as the child relates to the world around him or her, or they might only occur occasionally in specific situations. When the behaviour becomes a repeated pattern, parents and coaches may need to become sensitive to the existence of a problem.

Low self-esteem may be the cause when a child

- avoids a task or challenge without even trying, or gives up at the first sign of frustration. This often signals a fear of failure or a sense of helplessness
- cheats or lies to prevent losing a game or doing poorly
- shows signs of regression, acting babylike, or very silly. These types of behaviour invite teasing and name-calling from other youngsters, adding insult to injury
- becomes controlling, bossy, or inflexible to hide feelings of inadequacy, frustration, or powerlessness
- makes excuses ("The teacher is dumb") or downplays the importance of events ("I don't really like that game anyway"), using rationalizing to place blame on others or on external forces
- withdraws socially, losing or having less contact with friends, as school grades decline
- experiences changing moods, exhibiting sadness, crying, angry outbursts, frustration, or quietness
- makes self-critical comments, such as, "I never do anything right. " "Nobody likes me." "I'm ugly." "It's my fault." "Everyone is smarter than I am."
- has difficulty accepting either praise or criticism
- becomes overly concerned or sensitive about other people's opinions
- seems strongly affected by negative peer influence, adopting attitudes and behaviours like a disdain for school, cutting classes, acting disrespectfully, shoplifting, or experimenting with tobacco, alcohol, or drugs
- is either overly helpful or never helpful at home.

Modified from American Academy of Pediatrics *Caring for Your School-Age Child: Ages 5 to 12.* Used with permission.

How can coaches help build self-esteem in young children?▶

Building self-esteem means helping children to feel good about themselves. In the 3M Coaching Series *Getting Started in Coaching*, the Coaching Association of Canada (CAC) recommends that coaches help children develop confidence and self-esteem through the following ways:

1. Greet each child individually when they arrive for each session. Make them feel good about being there.
2. Show confidence in their ability to learn.
3. Offer activities that suit their level of development.
4. Encourage effort without always focusing on results.
5. Avoid elimination games and other activities that may add undue pressure. Create situations where there are lots of successes.
6. Be specific when telling them what you like about their effort or performance.
7. Use a smile, a nod, or a wink to acknowledge them.
8. Praise them for special things they have done. A 'pat on the back' means a lot.
9. Give them responsibilities. Involve them in making decisions and give each of them a chance to be a 'leader'. Alternate captains.
10. Ask them for their input and invite their questions.

When young people have fun and enjoy their experiences in sport, they stay involved longer and their self-esteem grows. In a video and pamphlet produced by the Canadian Centre for Ethics in Sport and the CAC, called *Coaching the Spirit of Sport: Building Self-Esteem*, parents, coaches, and teachers are shown how common sport scenes such as cutting athletes from the team or providing constructive feedback at practice can have a powerful effect upon a young person's self-image. The material, developed in consultation with Dr. Terry Orlick, also illustrates how to give constructive feedback after a win or loss. For example:

"Win or lose, positive feedback is extremely valuable. As you and the athletes enjoy the victory, point out the things that went well, identify areas for improvement, and help them draw out lessons as building blocks for future success."

"Following a loss, acknowledge an honest effort, highlight the positives, and ask the athletes to identify areas for improvement. Help them understand that a loss is an important learning experience and that their value as a person does not depend on whether they win or lose."

How do children interact with others? ▶

Young children think the world revolves around them and what they want. Until they are about five, most children are self-centred and egocentric. They expect other people to adapt to their needs.

It is not easy for young children to play cooperatively with others. They play beside, rather than with, each other. This is known as parallel play. Because they do not understand cooperative behaviour, they have difficulty playing team activities.

Children begin cooperative play between the ages of about six and nine. They develop friendships within small groups that slowly become more enduring. They often play in a world of make-believe and act out different parts. They begin to play roles and to understand what playing a role is all about.

Still, competition at this stage is a series of one-upmanships. Children compare themselves with their peers, striving to see who is best. They are concerned mainly with being the best at the expense of others.

When do children understand the meaning of long-term goals?

In the 1950s and 1960s, child psychologist Jean Piaget carried out a series of tests on children to explore their understanding of time. He discovered that many children, up to primary school age, have quite a poor understanding of time and are incapable of understanding long-term goals. As children pass through primary school, they begin to develop some concept of time.

With this in mind, instead of long-term goals, coaches should set challenging yet realistic short-term goals for youngsters: a swimmer could work on having a more forceful kick; a hockey player could improve the accuracy of a pass.

Goals like these are within a youngster's control. Dr. Stuart Robbins says practices should focus on immediate, simple goals. "Building endurance is not an achievement easily recognized by small children, but learning how to do a cartwheel or handstand is a noticeable accomplishment." Activities that produce immediate improvement help children to feel better about themselves.

The Mind Of A Child

References

Connell, R. (1993) Understanding the learner: guidelines for the coach. *Coaching Children in Sport*. London: E&FN SPON. pp. 79-90.

Haynes, D. (1989) Kids and sports: keeping it fun. *Today's Parent*. (February), pp. 35-36.

Kindra, G., Laroche, M., Muller, T. (1994) *The Canadian Perspective Consumer Behaviour*. Second Edition. Scarborough: Nelson Canada. p. 134.

Lee, M. (1994/95) Not mini-adults, part II: psychology. The psychological differences between children and adults. *Coaching Focus*. 27, (Winter), pp. 18-19.

Lee, M. (1993) Growing up in sport. *Coaching Children in Sport*. London: E&FN SPON. pp. 91-108.

Pridham, S., Hauswirth, M. (1992) *Success Stories*. Victoria: Sport Management Group. p. 26.

Schor, E. (1995) *Caring for your School-Age Child*. The American Academy of Pediatrics. New York: Bantam Books.

Sport Parent Survey. (1994) Ministry of Government Services Sports and Commonwealth Games Division. (July), p. 9.

Statistics Canada. (1992) *Sport Participation in Canada*. Ottawa: Canadian Heritage Sport Canada. p. 6.

Stewart, G. (1994) *Getting Started in Softball*. Gloucester: Coaching Association of Canada. pp. 8.

Part Five

Sport Injuries In Young Children

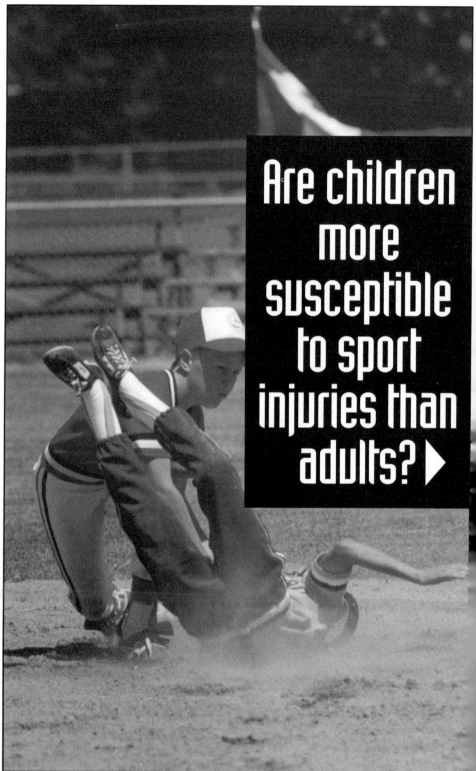

Are children more susceptible to sport injuries than adults?

T here is always a risk of injury associated with involvement in sport. Children are particularly prone to injury, even when they're not playing sport, because they tend to be more active than adults.

When children are injured during sport, the results can be more serious than for adults. Unlike adults, children's bones have growth plates — the soft cartilage near the ends of longer bones in the arms and legs — that are responsible for bone growth. In children, these plates may be the weakest link within the bone, making the bones susceptible to a fracture or break. Breaks involving the growth plate are serious and, if not treated properly, may interfere with growth.

Dr. William MacIntyre, an orthopedic surgeon at Ottawa's Children's Hospital of Eastern Ontario, says parents are often surprised to discover that a child has a fracture. They assume kids have rubber bones which will bend but will not break.

Growing may make children more susceptible to injury. Growth spurts can make some children more awkward as growing can throw off balance and coordination, even when the child has been previously agile.

Growing can also cause decreased flexibility for periods of time. Bones, as they grow, cause the muscles to become tighter than normal during growth spurts. In other words, as bones grow, they pull the muscles, which respond by constantly stretching until the muscle accommodates to the new bone length.

Young athletes are particularly vulnerable to injuries because the decrease in flexibility increases the risk of muscle imbalance problems. Training that overemphasizes one muscle group may also expose the growing athlete to injury.

Every child needs to exercise regularly to ensure normal physical growth and development. Youngsters who spend their free time watching TV or engaging in other sedentary pursuits may have impaired bone growth. Recent studies have shown that when weight-bearing physical activity is increased, bones become progressively denser and stronger. Children who take part in weight-bearing physical activity also have denser and stronger bones when they reach adulthood.

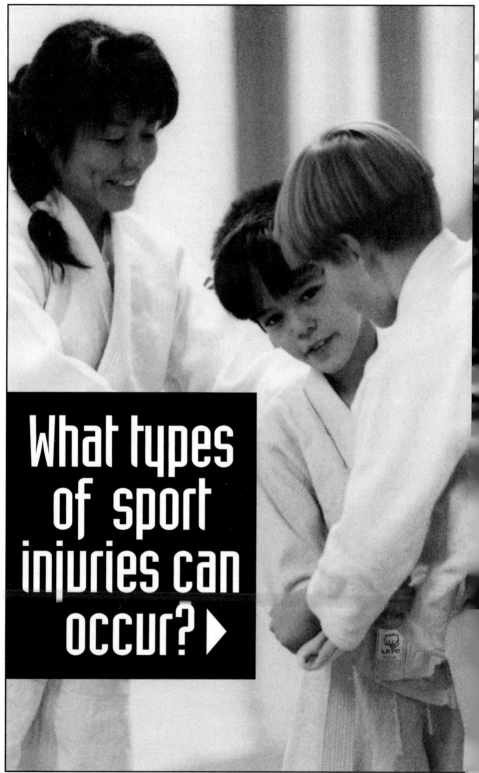

What types of sport injuries can occur?▶

There are two kinds of sport injuries — *acute* injuries and *overuse* injuries. Children have always suffered from acute injuries such as sprained ankles and broken arms. Today, however, because of intensive sport training at younger levels by some children, doctors are seeing a dramatic increase in overuse injuries.

Overuse injuries are caused by repeating the same techniques over and over again. Children may, in fact, be more susceptible to overuse injuries than adults because constantly repeating similar movements at a time when they are growing can create muscle imbalances around the joints.

ACUTE INJURIES
Broken bones in the upper body are common in children because their arm and wrist muscles are frequently weak. A simple fall can result in a fracture if the muscles aren't strong enough to absorb the impact for the bone. Even highly active children, who are fit from playing sports such as running or soccer, may not be physically fit in the upper body. Orthopedic surgeon William MacIntyre recommends that children be encouraged to do push-ups and chin-ups to strengthen muscles and prevent injury.

OVERUSE INJURIES
Children in organized sport who practise a technique over and over again risk developing overuse injuries. These commonly occur in the shoulder, elbow, knee, and ankle joints. Little League pitchers, for example, risk developing pain in their throwing arms.

One of the most common overuse injuries is patello-femoral knee pain, accounting for nearly one half of all knee pain seen in adolescents. Sport physiotherapist Lorraine Hendry of Ottawa, an expert in patello-femoral knee syndrome, says that children can develop pain around the knee cap in any sport where their bent knee moves against resistance. The syndrome is common during growth spurts when an imbalance in the muscle groups controlling the knee cap makes it tilt and rub against the wrong side of the thigh bone. The syndrome is often overlooked, but it can be corrected with early treatment such as proper stretching and strengthening exercises. If not promptly treated, the syndrome can lead to more serious knee injuries.

What are the most common sites of injury?

Cliff Patterson

T he knees bear the brunt of more injuries than any other part of the body. Knee injuries are particularly prominent when children become involved in organized sports such as soccer, ice hockey, football, or alpine skiing which involve a lot of turning and twisting or present the possibility of collision.

Ankle injuries are also very common. Children who participate in sports such as volleyball, basketball, and running face the risk of landing on an overturned ankle, resulting in a sprain or fracture. Coaches should pay particular attention to stretching the calf muscles and strengthening the muscles surrounding the ankle. Exercises that improve an athlete's balance, such as standing on one foot and rocking up on the toe and back on the heel, can strengthen ankle muscles and prevent injury.

How to treat an acute injury.
Begin treatment immediately. The RICE principle can be used as a treatment guide for all soft tissue injuries.
REST — Keep the child off the injured limb to allow healing to take place.
ICE — Apply ice for 10 to 15 minutes. Repeat at hourly intervals for at least 72 hours. Check the skin periodically to avoid ice burns.
COMPRESSION — Apply a tensor bandage through the day in the early stages. Remove it in the evening. Compression will decrease the swelling.
ELEVATION — Elevate the injured limb above the heart when possible. This will prevent pooling of fluid in the limb.

What are serious injuries in children's sport?

Head and neck injuries must always be taken seriously. So should growth plate injuries in children. A sudden violent force, which would cause a ligament injury in an adult, can cause a growth plate injury in a child because these parts are weaker than the ligaments.

Growth plate injuries are more common to contact or collision sports. One year-long study of 300 children involved in six different sports found five of eight growth plate fractures happened playing football. Though most growth plate injuries don't result in long-term problems, some may cause permanent damage to the bone, including shortness of the limb.

Other injuries could endanger the normal growth of a child. An adult could tear a muscle by extreme muscle contraction, yet a similar force could make the muscle pull away part of the bone in young children.

Undisplaced growth plate injuries are hard to detect on an x-ray. If an x-ray is read as normal and the youngster continues to limp with pain, the child should be reassessed before returning to sport.

Are some exercises harmful to growing muscles and bones?▶

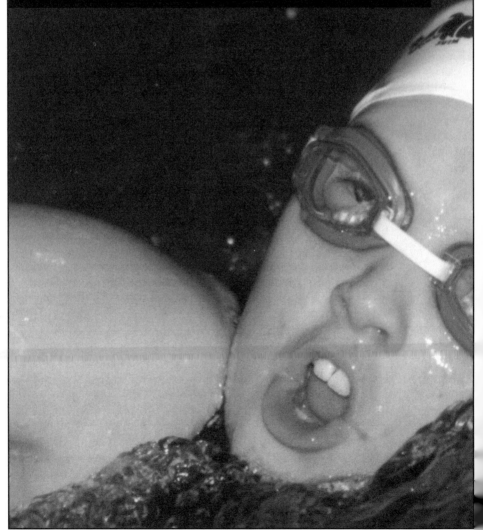

Swim Ontario

Most exercises are not harmful if performed properly and within certain limits. However, growing children should never lift heavy weights. Children have a natural tendency to push their limits, to see how fast they can run or how far they can climb. Finding out how much they can lift could be dangerous for the pre-adolescent. Under proper adult supervision, children can use light weights; that is, those they can comfortably lift 12 to 15 times. Excessively high repetition should also be avoided.

Overstretching or stretching a joint beyond its normal range of motion can be harmful for a youngster. Stretching is best done by the child itself after proper training. Sometimes when a coach or teammate helps a child stretch, they may stretch a joint beyond its normal range. This type of overstretching increases the laxity in the joint, making it more susceptible to injury.

In particular, overstretching the shoulder joint makes it prone to dislocation. This shallow joint has the most mobility of any of our joints. The soft tissue structures surrounding the joint have quite a bit of give, but they need strong muscles to maintain stability. When the shoulder joint is overstretched, the capsule and ligaments may no longer provide sufficient stability to prevent shoulder dislocations later on.

Competitive swimmers and gymnasts are particularly susceptible to shoulder problems such as tendinitis and dislocations. Tendinitis is caused by a combination of overuse and weak muscles. This type of injury is common in the shoulder, elbow, and ankle joints. In general, treatment for tendinitis is rest, applying an ice bag, and performing stretching and strengthening exercises — without overstretching.

Sports such as gymnastics, diving, figure skating, and weightlifting, where athletes are likely to perform hyperextensions of the lower back, can cause a defect in the lower spine in which one vertebrae slips forward onto the next lower vertebrae. Explosive landings in an arched position and back handsprings may result in a hyperextension injury of the lower back. Abdominal muscle strength is very important in trying to avoid hyperextension injuries to the lower back. Coaches should avoid putting children in a situation where they put stress on a hyperextended body joint.

How can parents and coaches prevent injuries?▶

The Ottawa Citizen

Sport physiotherapist Lorraine Hendry recommends these commonsense precautions to help maintain the safety of young children in sport.

- Provide a safe environment, using well-maintained equipment.

- Ensure that children are playing with others of their own size and ability, not squaring off against players who significantly outweigh them.

- Avoid performing harmful exercises like overstretching with a teammate or hyperextensions of the back.

- Avoid excessive repetition of sport techniques by involving children in a wide variety of sports. Encouraging youngsters to play a variety of sports and develop different skills reduces the risk of overuse injuries. Similarly, within the game itself, encourage each child to play different positions.

- Do not ask young athletes to perform beyond their capabilities. Poor conditioning and lack of fitness can lead to injuries. Just because kids are active doesn't necessarily mean they are fit.

- Recognize that body build or alignment problems such as bowed legs or flat feet may predispose a child to injury.

- Discourage children from sitting while their knees and thighs are rotated in and their feet are out to each side (see inset). This encourages the feet to turn inwards, making running difficult. Children usually begin this practice, known to practitioners as TV w-sitting, as early as age one or two. Cross-legged sitting should be encouraged.

Suzanne Beaulieu

- Choose sport programs that emphasize the four components of fitness — muscular strength, muscular endurance, cardiovascular endurance, and flexibility. A well-balanced, flexible body resists injury better than a weak, poorly-conditioned one.

- Begin every practice with a proper warm-up and stretching exercises and end with a proper cool-down including stretching exercises.

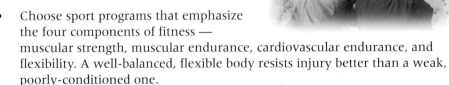

What is an effective warm-up and cool-down? ▶

When it comes to injury prevention, warming up and cooling down are an important part of playing the game. A coach should never simply tell a child to do the warm-up at the start of a practice. Children often don't know how to warm up properly. They need to do their warm-up exercises as a group and be given direction on what exercises to perform.

Every exercise session should begin with an activity that warms and loosens the muscles and connective tissues and raises the heart rate. A game of tag is not only fun, but also helps to warm the body and get the blood flowing. The body needs about five minutes of movement with about five to 10 minutes of stretching.

Following the warm-up, the coach should instruct the children in slow or static stretching. Holding stretches for 10 to 15 seconds allows the muscles to stretch to their greatest length. Bouncing during a stretch should be avoided.

A total body stretch starts from the head and moves down the body including the neck and chest, shoulders, the back, the groin, hamstrings or back of the thigh, quadriceps or front of the thigh, and the heel cords.

Practices should end with a proper cool-down to bring the heart rate back to normal and the body back to its normal temperature. Cool-down also prevents stiffness and sore muscles.

Youngsters should never just stop moving after a strenuous game or practice. A cool-down involves gradually slowing down the sport or activity, cooling down the body for approximately 10 minutes. This should be followed by more stretching. After exercise, the body is more flexible.

How to dress for safety.

When a child is active in sport, dressing safely is an important part of injury prevention. Here is some commonsense advice on how to dress for safety.

- Anything that dangles is dangerous. Ties should be removed from coats or jackets. Neckwarmers are safer than scarves.
- Wearing jewelry on the playing field is inappropriate. Remove rings, necklaces, and earrings.
- On hot summer days, cool, light-coloured clothing is recommended. Hats and sunscreen are a must. In winter, dressing in layers is best. If the child gets too hot, one layer can be peeled off.
- For indoor sports, footwear should be appropriate for the sport. High-cut running shoes are best for sports where there is a lot of twisting and turning.

What factors should be considered in purchasing protective equipment?▶

Suzanne Beaulieu

Protective equipment is designed to prevent injuries. Depending on the sport, children should wear a well-fitted helmet, mouthpiece, faceguard, padding, eye gear, protective cup, or other equipment appropriate for the sport.

Protective equipment is not a reason to relax the application of sport rules, says Dr. Stuart Robbins. Coaches have to be just as careful about applying the rules of the game when children are wearing protective equipment. Children should be warned not to take unnecessary risks when playing sports and reminded that wearing protective equipment doesn't make them invincible.

Many sport organizations and even some federal regulations will not allow young children to participate without protective equipment. In many provinces, cyclists are required by law to wear a bicycle helmet. Protective eyewear is absolutely essential in sports such as hockey and squash. Children should wear mouthguards if there is a possibility of collision or if they are playing sports with balls, bats, or sticks.

To do any good, equipment must fit and be used properly. A helmet won't do its job if it's pushed too far back on a child's head. Equipment such as ski bindings need to be properly adjusted to each child's height, weight, and level of ability in order to provide safety.

All sports equipment must be chosen to fit the child now. It should not be modified or altered except as specified by the manufacturer. Parents and coaches have a responsibility to examine the equipment regularly for fit and defects.

Beyond safety, kids should play sports in comfortable, well-fitting new or used equipment. Trying to save a little money buying skates to last for two years or using hand-me-downs that are too small may make a child's experience miserable.

References

Carmichael, D. (1986) Focus on junior sport: what every adult should know about children and sport. *Sports Coach*. 10(3), pp. 41-45.

Chambers, R.B. (1982) Orthopedic injuries in athletes (Ages six to 17). Hahn's and Pyke's implications for growth and development principles for practice and policy in junior sport. *Coaching Seminar Update*. Canberra, Australia: Sport and Recreation Branch. Department of Home Affairs and Environment. pp. 5-18.

Hendry, L. (1994) The adolescent athlete and patello-femoral knee pain. *Coaches Report*. 1(2), pp. 10-13.

Hendry, L., O'Hara, P., McGrath, P., Baxter, P., Leikin, L. (1994) The conservative management of patello-femoral knee pain in female adolescents—In Preparation.

Morrissey, D. (1994/95) Injuries in young people and their prevention. *Coaching Focus*. 27, Winter, pp. 20-22.

Wong Briggs, T. (1990) Injuries increase in organized sport. *USA Today*. September 10th.

Part Six

The Role Of Parents And Coaches In Sport

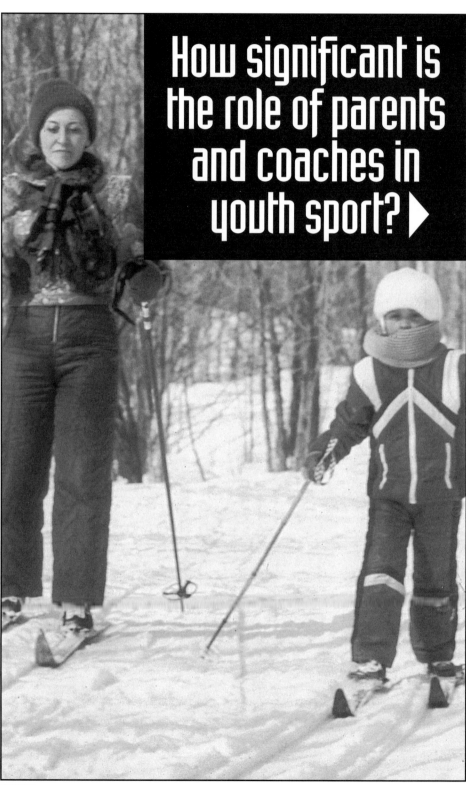

How significant is the role of parents and coaches in youth sport?

The success of a sport program depends primarily on the quality of adult leadership. Teachers, coaches, officials, spectators, and parents all affect the experience and determine to a large extent whether it will be positive.

However, of all the adults involved, parents and coaches are perhaps the most important. It's their attitudes, beliefs, and behaviours which undoubtedly affect the child the most.

The relationship between the coach and the young athlete is critical. How a coach teaches new skills, manages a practice, gives feedback, recognizes effort, and behaves with players and parents is essential to establishing a healthy environment.

Canada is very fortunate to have some of the world's best coaches working with our athletes. Over the last 25 years, the Coaching Association of Canada, in its quest to determine what makes a 'model coach', has developed a central theme — a good coach is someone who creates an environment that allows athletes to succeed. Former president Dr. Geoff Gowan says, "Good coaches build the confidence needed for athletes to believe in themselves so they can perform at their highest level."

The role of parents is to decide what a child's sport needs are, investigate the programs that are available, decide which ones are the most appropriate for the child's age and ability, estimate the quality of the youngster's experience, and decide whether a particular activity lends itself to a lifelong habit of exercise. Parents should also determine whether the coach's philosophy is compatible with their own personal values.

Very few children can participate in sport without the financial and emotional support of their families. Often, family arrangements are made around a child's sport commitments. Research shows that children are more likely to participate in sport if their parents do. A study commissioned by Sport Canada on sport participation by Canadians showed that a mother's participation had a greater effect than a father's on a child's likelihood of involvement.

What can be done when a parent misbehaves? ▶

Parents 'coaching' from the sidelines, criticizing the opposition, or verbally abusing officials and coaches are common examples of parents *misbehaving* in children's sport. Fortunately, the majority of parents and adult spectators do not engage in this sort of excessive behaviour.

Most parents spend their time silently watching the game or chatting with friends. However, one fanatical parent can ruin a child's experience and have a serious negative impact on the whole team.

Researchers have found that certain factors help to explain why some parents are intrusive. For example, the proximity of spectators to one another or to the players, familiarity with the game, and the closeness and importance of the game, as perceived by adults, are all factors that may indicate a greater inclination for parents to offer verbal comments or criticisms.[1]

Another factor is the tendency to value winning above all else. In this case, parents constantly focus on what they perceive to be mistakes players, officials, and coaches make, especially in the crucial last moments of a game.

In an article in *Sports Coach* called "The Odd Angry Parent: What Are The Coach's Options?", John Evans advises coaches who are dealing with disruptive parents that prevention is the best cure. He suggests holding an orientation meeting to inform parents about the program's philosophy and goals and what is expected of parents during a practice or game situation. Coaches who find themselves with a disgruntled parent should meet the parent after-hours to discuss the problem openly and point out the negative effect such behaviour is having on the child and possibly the team.

Parents who are kept busy may have fewer opportunities to complain. For some parents, it can be useful to be responsible for a task which may focus their efforts on the well-being of all of the children. Scoring, being team manager, keeping statistics, umpiring, or being equipment manager are all good possibilities.

Parents are also less likely to intervene if they believe that the children are in the hands of a knowledgeable coach. Factors such as experience and coaching qualifications are important in convincing parents that the child is well-supervised.

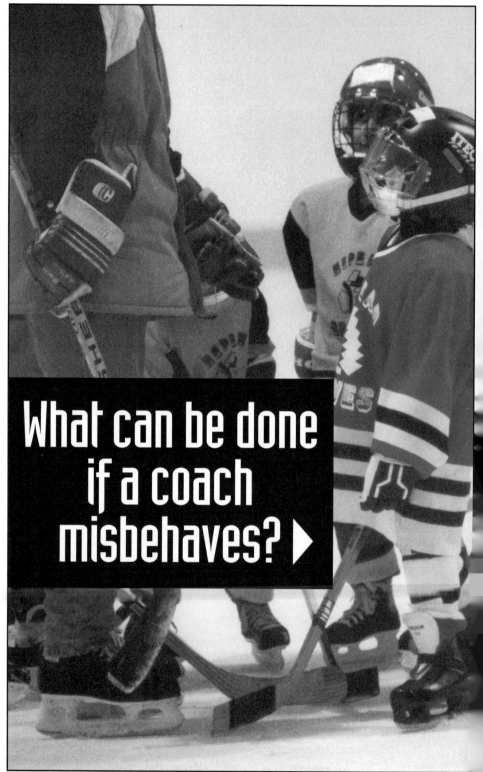

What can be done if a coach misbehaves? ▶

Most children have enormous respect for their coaches. According to one study, 96 per cent of young athletes stated that coaches were a greater source of influence on their behaviour than teachers, parents, or their peers. But when coaches encourage children to cheat or abuse them in any way, the impact can be serious.

Gaston Marcotte, a professor of physical education at Université Laval in Québec City, has been a very outspoken critic of the lax approach most sport clubs have to the selection and monitoring of coaches. He notes that the people who prepare the ice surfaces at hockey arenas have to be licensed and trained, but any volunteer can walk in off the street and coach a team without even a background check.

One problem that could occur in coaching is cheating. Parents who hear of coaches who encourage cheating should inform them that teaching children to cheat is unacceptable and should let the other parents know what is going on. If the coach denies or refuses to change the behaviour, parents can go to the convenor for action. If nothing is done, look for a better sport environment. Unfortunately, taking a child off the team is hard because you're penalizing the child instead of the coach.

Children are also vulnerable to sexual abuse by adults involved in sport. Sporting environments increase the potential for abuse. Sexual abusers find it easy to work in locker rooms and showers, on trips, and during tournaments. The traits that make children good athletes — obedience, pliability, an eagerness and willingness to please — also make them targets for sexual abuse. Children are afraid the coach will reject them if they say "no" to improper advances. As parents, be wary of situations that are inappropriate. For example, never let your child train alone or go to a coach's house unattended.

If possible, make sure another adult is involved in the coaching process. This means that contact with children is always in the presence of another adult. If individual coaching is required, make sure the room is open so the children can be seen by other people. Be sure that all touching is limited to what is strictly needed for proper coaching such as spotting or the correction of errors.

Verbal abuse is another problem that may occur in coaching. Coaches who value winning above all else may berate young children for missing a shot or not landing a jump. This type of behaviour is inappropriate for any coach — at any level of sport.

Why should coaches be certified?

H istorically, coaches were selected for their athletic accomplishments and the all-too-common belief that, "I played the sport for 20 years so I can surely coach it." Even though the attitude that 'coaching requires no special skills and anyone can do it' still exists, experts agree that today's coaches need training in order to be effective.

Sport administrators now recognize that understanding sport techniques is only one component of being a good coach. In order to do the job effectively, coaches need to know a great deal about children. How do children grow and develop? What can coaches do to build self-esteem? What is the best method to teach new skills?

Coaches are the most important link in providing a healthy sport experience. Good coaches balance a sound philosophy of coaching with high ethical standards and a solid understanding of skill learning, growth and development, and the needs of athletes. Parents should feel a moral responsibility to determine whether their children are in the hands of competent and ethical role models.

In sport, there is one recognized formal educational track — the National Coaching Certification Program (NCCP). This five-level program trains coaches from novice to master in more than 60 different sports. Over 600,000 coaches have participated in the program since its inception in 1974.

For coaches working at the community, school, or club level, the NCCP teaches the general principles of coaching such as how to plan a practice, how to motivate young children, and how to teach skills, as well as the sport-specific information on skills and drills, rules of play, strategy, and tactics. The Coaching Association of Canada (CAC), the national body which oversees the development of the program, works in collaboration with the federal and provincial/territorial governments, and national, provincial/territorial sport organizations to offer courses in local community centres, colleges, universities, and other host sites across Canada. Home study programs are also available.

Today, minimum levels of coaching certification are required by many sport organizations before coaches are certified to practice. The CAC recommends that all coaches, whether novice or master, be certified in the NCCP. If you are interested in becoming a coach, contact the CAC at the address listed at the beginning of this book.

What is a competent coach? ▶

John Krulic

The Coaching Association of Canada believes that a competent coach is one who has the appropriate knowledge, skills, and attitude to do the job effectively.

Good coaches must have a sound *knowledge* of coaching principles. They must understand the principles that apply to learning, training within a sport environment, and human development. They must understand the sport, its techniques, strategies, and tactics. And they need an understanding of athletes and their individual characteristics. This knowledge doesn't automatically come from participating in a sport for 20 years. Qualified coaches need to be trained to recognize and understand these important principles and to apply them on-the-field.

Many of the *skills* that good coaches apply can also be learned or refined. These include how to be a good leader, teacher, and administrator.

- **Leadership Skills.** Watching the game, you should be able to tell very quickly if the coach relates well and can manage the children effectively. Is the coach a good problem-solver? Can the coach motivate the group to work as a team? Does the coach recognize everyone's contribution and celebrate achievements? Does the coach set reasonable goals for the group in terms of age and ability? Is effort recognized as much as performance?

- **Teaching Sport Skills.** Because many elementary schools no longer provide children with a good grounding in sport skills, it is essential that the coach knows the fundamentals and is qualified to teach them to young children. A good coach helps players learn by explanation, demonstration, and practice. Does the coach communicate well with athletes? Does the coach crouch down to a child's eye level to give instructions? Is individual guidance provided even in a group setting? Are skills taught in a progressive manner and within a safe environment?

- **Organizational Skills.** A good coach does not have six children working like demons while the others do nothing. He or she moves easily from group to group, knowing what comes next. Is the coach well-organized? Are practices well-organized? Is there lots of opportunity for participation?

Coaches are figures of authority and role models. They should have the proper *attitude* toward sport that will instill values of sportsmanship and fair play. Does the coach put winning in perspective? Does the coach encourage children to respect the rules and to respect others?

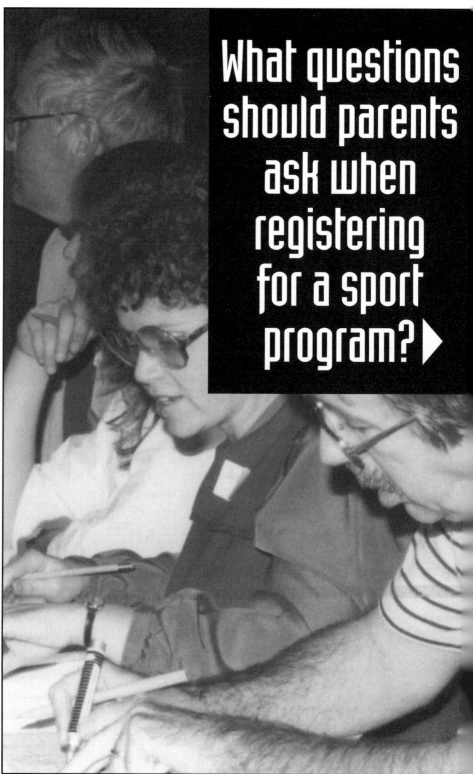

What questions should parents ask when registering for a sport program? ▶

S hopping around for a good sports program is worthwhile in the long run. A child's early exposure to sport lays the groundwork for participation in the years to come. When registering a child in a sports program, consider these questions:

1. Are the coaches certified in the National Coaching Certification Program? What coaching experience do they have?
2. Is there a policy of equal playing time?
3. Does the program emphasize the development of skills?
4. Are the play areas safe and well-maintained?
5. What is the ratio of practice-to-competition? For example, three or four practices to one game is appropriate for young children.
6. Are the groupings and teams suitable for safe and enjoyable activity?
7. Are there lots of opportunities for children to play?
8. Are youngsters encouraged and congratulated for good efforts?
9. Are the needs of the children taken into consideration? For example, are practices at a convenient time and place? Are they limited to a reasonable length of time? Will time demands prevent the children from participating in other activities and assuming other responsibilities?
10. Are safety rules adhered to during practices and games? Is appropriate equipment available? Are children matched with others of the same size?

Questions to ask youngsters after a game.

The first question parents usually ask their child after a game is, "Did you win?" Whether the answer is "Yes, we won" or "No, we didn't win," it doesn't really tell you anything about what the child has just experienced. Ask the right questions and learn from the answers

- Did you have fun?
- What was your favorite part of the game?
- What didn't you like about today's game or practice?
- What did you learn?
- What do you need to work on?
- Can I help you improve any skill?
- Were you nervous during the game today?
- What did the coach say after the game?
- Were you a good sport?

What should parents watch for during a game or practice? ▶

Sitting on the sidelines, parents and spectators are in a good position to determine whether the sport experience is a good one for children. Dr. Geoff Gowan, a former Olympic athletics coach, developed this checklist for parents.

Practices should be well-organized and purposeful. The coach should be in charge and well-prepared for practice. Equipment should be set up and the children organized quickly into groups to practise different skills.

Every practice should have a high level of activity and involvement for all children. Children don't like to stand around waiting for their turn to kick the ball. They should be active — most of the time!

Every practice should progress from known skills to new skills. After a proper warm-up, the children should begin familiar drills to improve or maintain their skills. Then the coach should build on these skills by introducing new ones to the group.

A good coach communicates clearly. A picture is worth a thousand words. New skills should be clearly introduced with a demonstration. If the coach notices the skill has not been absorbed, he or she should stop the practice and ask the children to watch while another demonstration is given as a reminder.

A good coach makes encouraging comments to the group. Coaches should encourage their charges by praising their efforts. Children like to be told they are doing a good job and working hard.

A good coach provides specific instruction to individual children. "Just try to open those fingers a bit more when you catch the ball, Gregory." "Watch where you're throwing that ball when you throw it to Caroline. Try and throw it right into her tummy. That's good. That's a lot better."

A good coach provides opportunities for feedback and questions from the children. Children should never be discouraged from asking questions.

A good coach lets everybody play. Sign up with a coach who believes everybody should play even if it means missing the playoffs. Everybody goes up to bat whether they are good batters or not.

A good coach has happy children. Children who enjoy working with a good coach leave practices happy and satisfied, ready to come back the next time.

Can officiating promote progress?

There's more to refereeing children's sports than blowing whistles. A referee who takes on the role of supplementary coach can make a significant difference to games played by young children. A good referee is more teacher than rule enforcer. He or she can give young players on-field lessons which they will carry through the game and into future games.

Referees control the way a game is played. They are there to help the game flow and to ensure it is played properly and fairly. Even at the World Cup, the highest level of international rugby, the referees continually talk to, warn, and advise the players to ensure as much continuity of play as possible without unnecessary stoppages.

In children's games, a referee who blows the whistle when an error is committed should not be afraid to stop the game and explain why the whistle was blown. "Pam, your tackle on Jane was unfair because you went in from behind. Next time, watch your approach."

Even for individual sports, officials and judges can take the opportunity to give pointers to young athletes. For example, a track and field official might explain to a long jumper how the jump is measured from the rear-most break in the sand to the take-off board.

What does fair play mean to a child?

Children know when something's not fair. You hear them say it all the time: "It's not fair. She started before the referee said, 'Go.'" But fair play doesn't just happen. It has to be deliberately taught and reinforced by the behaviour of coaches, parents, and teachers.

Children learn by example. From good role models, they learn respect for their opponents and understand that competition is meaningless when someone has an unfair advantage. If they understand the concept of fair play, children can experience the thrill of competition based on skill, performance, and the desire to win. Coaches and referees can use the rules of the game to explain fair competition. "Michel is off-side and if I hadn't blown the whistle, he would have had an unfair advantage."

Every game should end with a handshake — a symbol of good will, acceptance, and fair play.

Is there too much adult domination in children's sport? ▶

ost adults can remember shinny hockey and sandlot baseball. It was a time when children developed a true love of sport because they played for sheer enjoyment.

A lot of things have changed since those days. As Dr. Murray Smith writes in *Recreation Canada*, " ... adult involvement in kids' sports is deeper and more influential than it used to be. This deeper involvement has resulted in a shift in emphasis from helping 'where they could' to a pretty clear domination of kids' sport by adults."

Although unsupervised sport may have become almost a thing of the past, today's children should primarily be having fun in any sport they play, with winning and losing a by-product. Whatever the role of adults, it should always be encouraging, supportive, and positive.

The following comment by David Gey first appeared in *The Christian Athlete* in December, 1976 and was reprinted in *Joy and Sadness in Children's Sport* (1978). It reminds us that sport is for kids to enjoy.

> I believe the youth league idea is a great one with some minor changes: Put an eight-foot board fence around the playing area and only let the kids inside; take away all uniforms and let the kids wear street clothes; let them choose teams by the one potato, two potato system; let them play until it gets dark or until the kid with the ball goes home.

To that, Dr. Geoff Gowan adds the final note. "Let us not as adults take the game away from children and mould it to adult standards. Let us encourage children to enjoy being active through enjoyable play and appropriately designed competition which meets their needs. If we do this, we will have made an important contribution to their development through sport."

Reference Notes

1   Evans, J. (1993) The odd angry parent: what are the coach's options. *Sports Coach.* (April-June), pp. 13-18.

References

Deshaies, P., Vallerand, R., Guerrier, J.P. (1984) *La connaissance et l'attitude des jeunes sportifs Québécois face à l'esprit sportif.* Québec: À la Régie de la sécurité dans les sports du Québec.

Evans, J. (1993) The odd angry parent: what are the coach's options. *Sports Coach.* (April-June), pp. 13-18.

Gey, D. (1976) *The Christian Athlete.* Philadelphia.

Martens, R. (1978) *Joy and Sadness in Children's Sports.* Champaign: Human Kinetics. p. 113.

Logan, S. (1994) Why coaches should be certified. *Nova Scotia Sport.* pp. 16.

Randall, L., McKenzie, T. (1987) Spectator verbal behaviour in organized youth soccer: a descriptive analysis. *Journal of Sport Behaviour.* 10(4) pp. 200-211.

Schor, E. (1995) *Caring for your School-Age Child.* The American Academy of Pediatrics. New York: Bantam Books.

Smith, M. (1975) Adult domination in kids' sports. *Recreation Canada.* 33, p. 51.

Statistics Canada. (1992) *Sport Participation in Canada.* Ottawa: Canadian Heritage. Sport Canada. p. 6.